Business Intelligence Using Smart Techniques

Business Intelligence Using Smart Techniques

Environmental Scanning Using Text Mining and Competitor Analysis Using Scenarios and Manual Simulation

Charles Halliman

Revised Edition

[IU]
Information Uncover
Houston, Texas

Information Uncover, Houston 77089
© 2001, 2006, 2009 by Charles Halliman
First edition published 2001
Paperback edition published 2006
Revised edition published 2009

For information, contact Information Uncover
http://www.InformationUncover.com

10 9 8 7 6 5 4 3

Publisher's Cataloging-in-Publication
(Provided by Quality Books, Inc.)

Halliman, Charles.
    Business intelligence using smart techniques :
environmental scanning using text mining and competitor
analysis using scenarios and manual simulation / Charles
Halliman. — Rev. ed.
    p. cm.
    Includes bibliographical references and index.
    LCCN: 2008932804
    ISBN-13: 978-0-9674906-6-3
    ISBN-10: 0-9674906-6-9

    1. Business intelligence. 2. Business planning.
I. Title.

HD38.7.H345 2009   658.4'7
                                    QBI08-600321

Contents

Contents

Contents

Preface

This is a revised edition of the book, *Business Intelligence Using Smart Techniques: Environmental Scanning Using Text Mining and Competitor Analysis Using Scenarios and Manual Simulation*. Although we didn't feel that the first edition needed to be completely rewritten, we did feel that the first edition needed some key revisions and additions. In this revised edition for example, we address modifications we've made to our business intelligence techniques, we talk some about the link between business intelligence and strategic management, and we increase the references in the bibliography.

We also replace "company" with "organization" in many instances in this revised edition. We do this to emphasize that the methods shown in this book are applicable to all industries, including those industries containing organizations not generally referred to as "companies." For instance, we are now using the methods discussed in this book to analyze information associated with the health care industry—specifically, the segment of the health care industry containing organizations that provide bariatric, or weight loss, products or services.

As stated in the first edition, this book will show you how to examine business environmental information to find opportunities and threats. The ability to examine environmental information has always been desirable and useful. The ability has been especially useful in **SWOT** analysis where an organization's **strengths** and **weaknesses** are analyzed, in conjunction with the **opportunities** and **threats** the organization may experience.

The ability to examine business environmental information is more desirable and even necessary today, since information flows so quickly and in abundance. This quick flow of abundant information gives a prepared competitor an opportunity to gain a competitive edge.

There are various publications addressing the value of business intelligence in business strategy (Howson 2007, 92). And there are publications emphasizing the importance of business intelligence in strategic management (Fahy 2002, 5). Portions of these publications stress the significance of actionable information, which is information you can act on.

In order to create actionable information, you must be able to analyze information or engage in some form of knowledge discovery. Analyzing information and engaging in knowledge discovery are the kinds of activities that allow you to uncover opportunities and threats.

We view the discovery of opportunities and threats as knowledge discovery. We should note that some in the knowledge discovery field may believe that the discovered knowledge should be "previously unknown" by everybody and "truly new." But opportunity and threat business-related information is not necessarily previously unknown or truly new.

Preface

However, awareness of the implications of the information may be limited to a few people. And if used properly, the information may be "unknown enough" and "new enough" to improve an organization's competitive position. Information that may be used to improve an organization's competitive position is the sort of information we want to identify using the techniques shown in this book.

There is an abundance of publications addressing data mining techniques and their use as an aid in knowledge discovery in mostly-numeric databases. There are fewer publications addressing text mining where data mining-like techniques are used as an aid in the discovery of knowledge in mostly-text databases.

There are reasons for this. Text mining, in general, is more difficult to perform than data mining. Text tends to be presented in less structured form than mostly-numeric data. While numbers generally have definite meanings, text consisting of words, phrases, and sentences can have indefinite or inexact meanings. And it is generally easier to draw conclusions from numeric data than from text. Thus, there are more data mining projects to write about than text mining projects.

We use text mining to identify business-related "concepts." Although text mining is relatively new, the need to examine the business environment for opportunities and threats has been recognized for many years. In this book, we use text mining to identify and extract concepts related to business opportunities and threats. We use visualization methods to aid in analyzing these concepts.

Scenario and simulation methods have been used for many years. These methods help you imagine the future and determine what events might occur. These methods also help you determine how you might best manage possible future events. Many scenario and simulation methods require the use of a computer. The method described in this book does not. Many scenario and simulation methods require a lot of time and effort to establish the scenario and simulation exercise. Again, the method described in this book does not. Our method uses forms containing hand-checkable "boxes" (you simply put a check mark or "x" next to your chosen strategic option) to facilitate the scenario and simulation process.

In our method, we first determine the dominant environmental force impacting an industry. We assume that this force will help create conditions that will greatly influence the industry's future environment. We then do industry analysis presupposing the existence of environmental conditions usually associated with the dominant environmental force.

We investigate competitors identified in competitor-related concepts derived from our text mining efforts. We follow this investigation with scenario and simulation analyses. Based on the results of these analyses, we choose business strategies. These strategies include actions that can be taken by an organization to improve its business position.

The text mining and the scenario and simulation analysis methods discussed here are motivated by real projects the author has dealt with as a management consultant, as a manager, and as an engineer. The text analysis (or text mining) software described in this book was written to help the author quickly arrive at business intelligence results.

The methods shown in this book have been useful to us. We hope they will be useful to you. If you have comments or questions concerning the material presented in this book, please leave your comments or questions at http://www.InformationUncover.com.

Acknowledgments

I have not tried to list every person who influenced the contents of this book. In order to do that, I would need to go back more than thirty years and list engineers, software programmers, analysts, managers, business strategists, mentors, employees, and a whole host of people who have influenced my knowledge and experience. And I don't have the space to do that.

However, I do want to acknowledge the receipt of helpful comments from people who were good enough to take some time to look over all, or parts, of the first edition's manuscript, or all, or parts, of the revised edition's manuscript. These people are William Acar, Pieter Adriaans, Mary Ellen Bates, Eric Bloedorn, William Crowley, Peter Schwartz, Lesley Sprigg, Mark Wasson, and last but not least, my wife Linda. She is my biggest supporter and best critic.

All these people really do deserve my thanks. And I thank them for their contributions. I would like to state, of course, that any errors in this book are mine and are not the fault of any of the people, mentioned above, who kindly provided me with helpful comments.

Warning-Disclaimer

The information presented in this book is provided without any expressed or implied warranty. We believe the information to be accurate as of this book's publication date. However, the information is always subject to correction and update. Therefore, we do not guarantee that the information in this book is accurate or complete. And we are not liable for any profit loss, business loss, or other damages that may come as a result of errors or defects in this book.

Introduction

Business organizations need adequate information to operate properly and to achieve success. Today, business organizations are confronted with an explosion of business information. And if a business organization employs established methods to efficiently and effectively use the massive amounts of available information, that organization can gain a competitive advantage.

This book is about obtaining and analyzing organization-external business information, and using that information to help an organization meet its objectives. Examining the business environment for business information is sometimes called environmental scanning. The term environmental scanning was probably first mentioned in a broadly available publication authored by Francis Joseph Aguilar.

His Harvard dissertation on environmental scanning received the Columbia University doctoral dissertation prize in 1966. The title of the dissertation was *Scanning the Business Environment*. The dissertation was revised and published in book form during 1967 (Aguilar 1967).

In environmental scanning, the environment is broken up into sectors so that you can analyze each sector's information for strategic implications (Georgantzas and Acar 1995, 47). In our environmental scanning method, we divide the external environment into forces and analyze distributions and trends associated with those forces. We convert the distributions, trends, and underlying business information concepts into business intelligence that can provide insight into opportunities and threats.

We extract relevant information concepts from news sources that present the key opinions, actions, and expectations of influential industry-related environmental players. We create graphic pictures (or charts) of industry-related U.S. environmental forces, including competitor activities. We then analyze the charts and the extracted concepts to determine opportunities and threats.

This book puts the reader inside a fictional organization as a strategic analyst. The reader gets an opportunity to see how business information can be "mined" and analyzed. Text mining as a method for scanning business text is discussed, and scenario and simulation analysis as a technique for analyzing a competitor's activities is explained. The reader gets a good feel for environmental scanning, text mining, scenario and simulation analysis, and competitor analysis.

The chapters are laid out as follows: Chapter 1 describes data mining, text mining, the data warehouse, and the text warehouse. Chapter 1 also defines the environmental forces we scan for using text mining. An overview of our process and software used for the text mining described in this book is given in this chapter. Chapter 1 introduces information extraction as a special form of text mining. The definition of a "concept" as used in our information identification and extraction method is also discussed.

Chapter 2 discusses the air bag systems industry. This industry is used as our example-analysis industry. The air bag systems industry scanning results obtained as a product

Introduction

of our text mining methods, discussed in chapter 1, are shown in chapters 2, 3, 5, and 6. These results include environmental forces concepts and visualization charts for each of the ten years beginning with 1989 and ending in 1998.

Chapter 3 presents the notion of strategically capable competitors. These are organizations (or potential organizations) that are (or may be) able to compete in the business environment. We discuss strategic relevance as a measure of an article's competitor-related content. We discuss competitor-related concepts. And we discuss the methods we use to isolate the important strategically capable competitors.

Chapter 4 discusses business analysis methods. Our scenario and simulation method is among the methods introduced in this chapter. Also covered in chapter 4 are typical business strategies and typical business objectives that organizations establish as part of their mission. Chapter 5 evaluates real industry-related information using methods discussed in chapter 4.

Chapter 6 shows how competitor-related information can be readily exploited using scenario and simulation analysis. We establish twenty scenarios based on competitor-related concepts derived from text mining results. We then perform simulations based on these scenarios.

This book draws from the author's experience as a management consultant, a business information seminar leader, a manager at a Fortune 500 company, and a National Aeronautics and Space Administration (NASA) engineer. This book also draws from research done by experts in knowledge discovery, business strategy, and business information analysis.

You should read this book from beginning to end. You should read this book if you are interested in business strategy, strategic management, or business information analysis. And you should read this book if you are interested in environmental scanning, simulation and scenario analysis, or knowledge discovery in business-related text.

Chapter 1   Environmental Forces and Text Mining

BOOK OVERVIEW

Business intelligence can involve a broad array of ideas and opinions. It can mean anything and everything having to do with analyzing and using business information. And it can mean any information that helps an organization gain some insight into its business present or business future. For us, business intelligence is any information that reveals opportunities and threats that motivate an organization to take some action.

We consider business intelligence to be at the heart of strategic management. We see strategic management as the broader process of analyzing an organization's environment, establishing business objectives, and planning and engaging in activities to meet those objectives. Moreover, we believe that being able to analyze business information to arrive at business intelligence is key to effective strategic management.

We introduce text mining as a technique to scan and help evaluate large amounts of organization-external business text. (This technique commonly makes use of specially designed software.) Evaluating large amounts of business text is necessary to ascertain trends, distributions, and complex industry-related forces interactions. Evaluating large amounts of business text can give you a good idea of what your competitors are doing now and what they might do in the future.

We demonstrate how text mining methods can be used to make useful business information readily available. And we show how, once information is available, information analysis techniques, especially scenario and simulation, can effectively convert the information into actions beneficial to your organization. We don't just talk about how text mining and business information analysis can be used theoretically. We illustrate the delivery of text mining results and we demonstrate the analysis of those results.

We focus on two areas: The first area consists of external environmental forces. (We will use "environmental forces" to mean organization-external environmental forces in this book.) We define environmental forces as events that can cause an organization to achieve or fail to achieve a business objective. Environmental forces include the actions, opinions, and expectations of those who influence an industry. An organization's success, to a significant extent, depends on how the organization can deal with environmental forces (Stoffels 1994, xiii). We identify environmental forces by scanning or examining business text. We extract these forces and analyze them to determine how they can affect an organization. We perform a large part of the environmental forces analysis using visualization charts.

The second area of focus consists of the competitor forces that are a part of the environmental forces. We look at the competitor forces to determine how they can affect an organization. We employ specially designed forms to facilitate the competitor analysis process. The competitor analysis culminates with scenario and simulation exercises. Although competitor forces are part of the environmental forces, we look at competitor forces separately from other environmental forces because competitors can exert some of the strongest forces within the business environment. Understanding competitors and the forces they exert through their activities can enable an organization to greatly improve its tactics and strategy.

We focus on ten key environmental force types that affect an organization. These force types are as follows: regulatory forces, litigation forces, political forces, governmental forces, technology forces, collaborative forces, marketing forces, foreign forces (foreign business forces, to be more specific), management forces, and competitor forces.

Five competitor forces exist within an organization's business environment. The forces are these: an organization's direct rivals, suppliers for the industry, buyers for the industry's products or services, potential entrants to the industry, and organizations that offer a substitute product or service for an organization's product or service (Porter 1980, 3). The idea that these five forces comprise the competitive environment provides a foundation for understanding competitor activities.

A goal of any organization ought to be to gain access to information that can be analyzed rapidly to provide intelligence to the organization. The intelligence might include knowledge of the present and some very educated guesses about the future.

With the use of text mining tools, it is possible to identify and extract business concepts containing useful intelligence from text that conforms to a set of criteria. Some of the concepts can be analyzed to gain insight into the distribution and trends of environmental forces. And some of the concepts can be analyzed to gain insight into competitor activities. Scenario and simulation analysis is one of the tools that can provide this insight. Scenario and simulation analysis can be used to determine how an organization can make the best use of opportunities. The analysis can also be used to determine what action an organization should take to avoid potential threats from environmental forces—especially competitor forces.

We show you the results of applying text mining methods to a real industry. That industry is the air bag systems industry. We have created a fictional organization called **Mythical Air Bag Materials** that is assumed to be owned and operated by the readers and author of this book. We will assume that our organization makes air bag fabric. This fabric is the part of the air bag system that is inflated during an automobile accident.

We look at environmental forces affecting our organization and analyze the impact of these forces. We decide how those forces may shape future environments. We then use scenario and simulation analysis to determine appropriate responses to competitor actions assuming a specific environment. And we examine business strategies for our organization that may maximize opportunities and minimize threats within the assumed environment.

BUSINESS ENVIRONMENTAL FORCES

An environmental force is an event that can cause your organization to achieve or fail to achieve a business objective or business goal. Environmental forces include the actions, opinions, and expectations of those entities that can influence an industry. Those entities include competitors, business leaders, political organizations, the government, and other business environment players who influence an industry.

Examining business information associated with the business environment's major forces gives your organization the opportunity to innovate and try to cause as many of the forces as possible to work to your organization's benefit. If, for example, there appears to be some great new technology in your external environment that can help your organization, it has a chance to try to obtain that technology. Or your organization has an opportunity to change the rules of the game by introducing a better, different technology.

If there are political forces at work in your business environment, you have a chance to take advantage of those forces. For example, if you feel that political forces will cause new governmental regulations to be put in place, you have an opportunity to possibly influence those regulations so they will work more in your favor.

Key Environmental Forces

You should assess environmental forces for dominance. The environmental elements that exert the most force can affect your organization in positive or negative ways. And you may need to adjust your business objectives to the dominant environmental force to increase your organization's competitive edge. Based on our analysis, we concluded that the following ten force types represent the key environmental forces:

- **Governmental Forces ("GOV" in figures 1.1–1.6 and in figures 2.1–2.21)**

    These include government-run investigations and other activities that might lead to government-sanctioned guidelines, standards, regulations, and the like.

- **Regulatory Forces ("REG" in figures 1.1–1.6 and in figures 2.1–2.21)**

    These include regulations put in place by governmental agencies.

- **Political Forces ("POL" in figures 1.1–1.6 and in figures 2.1–2.21)**

  These include nongovernmental forces that directly influence governmental activities. For example, an action taken by a powerful nongovernmental group (such as a highly respected consumer organization) can be a political force.

- **Technology Forces ("TEC" in figures 1.1–1.6 and in figures 2.1–2.21)**

  These include technology, research, development, engineering approaches, new processes, and important innovative ideas.

- **Management Forces ("MAN" in figures 1.1–1.6 and in figures 2.1–2.21)**

  These include management changes such as hiring high-powered management talent or firing a manager. These also include managers' activities.

- **Collaborative Forces ("MER" in figures 1.1–1.6 and in figures 2.1–2.21)**

  These include mergers, acquisitions, partnerships, joint ventures, and agreements made between organizations.

- **Litigation Forces ("LEG" in figures 1.1–1.6 and in figures 2.1–2.21)**

  These include lawsuits that have been filed against or by an organization, indictments against an organization, and other litigation activities in which an organization might be involved.

- **Marketing Forces ("MAR" in figures 1.1–1.6 and in figures 2.1–2.21)**

  These include activities associated with the product or service price, promotion, and distribution of the product or service.

- **Foreign Forces ("FOR" in figures 1.1–1.6 and in figures 2.1–2.21)**

  These include import and export activities with respect to foreign countries—Japanese organizations selling cars in America, or American organizations selling computers in Europe, for example.

- **Competitor Forces ("COM" in figures 1.1–1.6 and in figures 2.1–2.21)**

  These include business organizations (or entities that can act like business organizations) whose actions can influence the industry—direct rivals, suppliers, buyers, organizations providing substitute products or services, or possible entrants to the industry.

Missing Forces

Two forces commonly included in key environmental forces are social and economic forces. We chose not to include these two forces, at least explicitly, in our list of key environmental forces. This is because keywords and phrases which explicitly characterize these forces (words like "needs," "wants," and "attitudes" for the social force, and words and phrases like "interest rates," "inflation," and "unemployment rates" for the economic force) are not typically found in representative numbers in most industry text.

However, these forces are often embedded in other forces. Social forces sometimes show up as political forces (for instance, special interest groups can be political forces). Social forces are also sometimes indicated in litigation forces (lawsuits for example). And social and economic forces can show up as market forces (changes in demographics for instance). So, even though we don't represent social and economic forces explicitly in our set of forces, the effects of social and economic forces are usually accounted for implicitly in the above ten force types.

DATA MINING AND TEXT MINING

There is a lot of talk today about data mining and how data mining methods are used to analyze corporate data. (In this book, the word "data" refers to a collection of elements where most of the elements are numeric in nature.) The data mining process goes something like this: Operational data that have been collected over a period of time by an organization and stored in a corporate database are moved to another database. That database is called a data warehouse (Adriaans and Zantinge 1996, 26). The contents of that warehouse are analyzed using data mining methods (especially software-related methods) to help discover new knowledge. The organization performing the analysis then uses the new knowledge to try to improve its business tactics or strategy.

Many definitions of data mining are associated with the notion of discovering new knowledge in huge databases. That new knowledge is used to make business decisions. Many text mining definitions, unlike many data mining definitions, aren't very specific. Often, text mining definitions leave you with a fuzzy impression of what constitutes text mining.

Some text mining discussions stress the importance of "discovering new knowledge." And the new knowledge is expected to be new to everybody. From a practical point of view, we believe that business text should be "mined" for information that is "new enough" to give an organization a competitive edge once the information is analyzed. We don't believe that the text mining necessarily discovers the knowledge. We believe that the analysis of the "mined" information is where the knowledge is discovered. A definition that supports this belief is shown below.

What Is Text Mining?

Text mining is the process of identifying concepts in, and extracting concepts from, unstructured text in document collections using methods (including specially designed software) that permit further analysis of the concepts. These concepts, which include ideas, issues, facts, opinions, rumors, and conjecture, may represent new knowledge or actionable information. Distribution analysis, trend analysis, and if-then rules are among the methods used to assess the concepts. And "new knowledge" is information that is "new enough" to help an organization improve its competitive position.

Although the above definition of text mining is similar to common definitions of data mining, the text mining definition does have a slightly different emphasis. "Unstructured" and "further analysis" are included in the text mining definition, making the text mining definition different from common characterizations of data mining. The word "unstructured" is in the text mining definition to emphasize that text mining must deal with something that has little or no structure—at least not the kind of structure that would make it easy to count and compare items of interest. "Further analysis" is in the text mining definition because direct human involvement is often a necessary component of the overall text analysis process. Many times, some person must scrutinize the text to get at the heart of the meaning of the text.

The Data Warehouse and the Text Warehouse

The data warehouse and the text warehouse are special kinds of databases. Before we talk about what a data warehouse is, and how we define a text warehouse, let's get a good feel for what a database is.

What Is a Database?

A database is a collection of elements which can include numbers, text, videos, sounds, and almost any kind of information that can be categorized. The capability to easily access individual elements within a database is one of its special characteristics. The elements within a database are stored in records. Each record is broken up into fields. A field is a predesignated slot set aside for the assignment of specific pieces of specific kinds of information (Kleiner 1999).

When most people think of databases, computer databases come to mind. However, databases do not have to reside on computers. The hard copy, as well as the computerized form of the white pages of a telephone book, is a database. And if all the fields within each record of the telephone book are filled in correctly, each record contains a name, an address, and a phone number. The parts of the name, the phone number, and the address have associated fields. In the hard copy form of the telephone-book database, records are laid out alphabetically making manual access to a specific record possible.

The text in the telephone-book fields is somewhat structured since well-defined text is assigned to the fields. For example, the name-fields are either empty or contain names if the contents of the fields are correct.

There are several types of databases. One type is the text database. A text database is a database that contains mostly text. While some of the text in most text databases is structured (systematically laid out), most of the text is usually unstructured. As an example, let's consider a design for a text database that is to contain nothing but articles from different newspapers.

One way of constructing the text database is as follows: Assign each article to a separate record; assign the newspaper name to a field within the record; assign the date of the newspaper publication to a field within the record; assign the article's headline to a field within the record; and finally, assign the body of the article to a field within the record. While the information in the date field and the information in the headline field are somewhat structured, most of the text in the body field, generally the largest field, is unstructured.

What Is a Data Warehouse?

A data warehouse is a computerized database of data taken mostly from an organization's operational database sources. It is generally felt that the data within a data warehouse should possess the following characteristics: The data should have a time stamp, meaning that each piece of data should have an associated time; the data should not be updated (the data should look as they did when assigned a time); the data should be subject oriented, meaning that the data should be organized using industry or business terms (such as services, products, distributors, buyers and marketing); and the data should be described in terms that are used consistently within the organization. If one department within an organization is using a set of codes or descriptors to label some piece of data, that usage should be consistent throughout the organization (Cabena et al. 1997, 19).

A data warehouse contains structured data. This means that you know what's where and what the data mean. For example, if there is a zip code field, you expect certain types of numbers to be in the field. And you know the possible magnitudes of the numbers in the field.

With its well-defined fields, its time stamp feature, and the absence of data field updates, a data warehouse can provide a means for discerning previous customer buying patterns as one of its capabilities. Knowing these patterns might enable you to estimate when and what customers might buy in the future. Warehoused data might help you determine if an ethnic or age group is more likely to purchase a product or service. Or warehoused data might help you determine if unknown purchasing relationships are gender based.

Chapter 1

What Is a Text Warehouse?

Inspired by the data mining and data warehouse descriptions discussed above, we define a text warehouse as follows: A text warehouse is a collection of "articles" taken from newspapers, wire services, radio or TV transcripts, newsletters, marketing reports, and other sources, and placed in a mostly-text computerized database. Each article must have a time stamp and no article can be updated.

A text warehouse domain is a subset of the warehouse. The domain contains similar articles. To be in a domain, an article must contain at least one word or phrase from a set of keywords or phrases that define the domain. And words and phrases used to describe domain concepts must be used consistently within all articles in the domain.

An article, by the way, is any text that contains at least one complete sentence. (Our text mining goal is to find business-related opportunities and threats associated with environmental forces, including competitor activities. We have found that complete sentences, as well as the other components of our text warehouse definition, are necessary to meet our goal.)

For us, a domain is a set of articles related to a topic. In this book, the topic, and thus the domain, is the air bag systems industry. Accordingly, every article in the air bag systems industry domain must contain at least one instance of one of the following words: air bag, air bags, airbag, airbags, air-bag or air-bags. This requirement insures that each of the articles is a relevant article.

The stipulation that words and phrases describing concepts be used consistently within different articles is difficult to meet. However, in business articles there are keywords and phrases that most business writers use to express certain business concepts. We show below many of the keywords and phrases that we believe are used to express these concepts.

Environmental Forces Keywords and Phrases

We established over fifty keywords (or keyword roots, or derivatives) and phrases to identify business concepts associated with the ten force types discussed above. Here are many of the keywords and phrases associated with the force types:

- The **"GOV"** keywords are government related words (or derivatives or roots) such as "government," "federal," "agenc," "council," "admin," "Commission," "commissioner," "senate," and "congress." These words or roots usually indicate some governmental entity.

- The **"REG"** keywords are regulation related words (or derivatives or roots) such as "regulation," "regulatory," "regulating," and "regulated." These words imply that some governmental agency is regulating, or about to regulate, some component of an industry.

- The **"POL"** keywords are political related words such as derivatives of "politic" or derivatives of "lobby." These are words that give you some idea of how nongovernment political organizations are responding to their members, the public, or corporations, and how the organizations are influencing the government. Following the activities of political organizations (the AARP or the American Association of Retired Persons, for example) can provide you with some warning as to what kind of regulations the government might put in place.

- The **"TEC"** keywords are technology related words (or derivatives or roots) such as "technology," "scien," "engineer," "developmental," "design," "develop," "patent," and "research."

- The **"MAN"** keywords are management related words (or derivatives or abbreviations) such as "ceo," "manager," "executive," and "exec." These words indicate a discussion about a manager's actions, or an organization's actions that affect a manager. An organization could be replacing one of its managers with a new manager, for example. The **"MAN"** keywords might indicate actions a manager is taking. If there are a lot of management changes in the industry, the words might indicate turmoil in the industry.

- The **"MER"** keywords or phrases consist of collaboration related words (or derivatives or roots) such as "alliance," "partnership," "joint venture," "acquisition," and "merger." In general, in the environmental forces analysis, we make no distinction between acquisitions, mergers, or alliances. We simply assume that when these and similar words are mentioned, it indicates that there will be a transfer, or sharing, of technology, management, financial resources, or some other business resource. (In competitor analysis, however, we should note that we do make a distinction between an organization engaged in a merger or acquisition and an organization engaged in some other collaborative activity. We show this distinction in our competitor-related if-then rules that we discuss in chapter 3.)

- The **"Leg"** keywords are litigation related words (or derivatives or roots) such as "judge," "suit" (as in lawsuit), "sue," "legal," "appellate," "plaintiff," "malpractice," and "indict." These words imply that some organization is now in legal trouble, or might be in legal trouble in the future.

- The **"MAR"** keywords are marketing related words (or derivatives or roots) such as "market," and words derived from the word "market." These include words such as "marketing" and "marketplace."

- The **"FOR"** keywords are foreign country related words (or derivatives) such as "Europe," "international," "export," and "import." These words might let you know if U.S. organizations see opportunities in foreign organizations. Also, these words might let you know if foreign organizations see opportunities in the U.S.

- The **"COM"** keywords are organization-indicator words (or derivatives or abbreviations) such as "corp," "corporation," "inc.," "co.," and "supplier." These words help you locate (or discover) organizations that offer substitutes for your product or service; organizations that are suppliers within your industry; organizations that are buyers within your industry; organizations that are potential entrants to your industry; or organizations that are direct rivals to your organization.

We should note that individual keywords or phrases don't necessarily contain information by themselves. In most cases, it is also the text around the keyword or the relationship between the different keywords or phrases in the text that is important. We illustrate this in chapter 2 with our concept analysis and in chapter 3 with our discussion of using if-then rules to find organizations with strategic capability.

Also, we should note that while the above set of keywords has had to be tweaked, from time to time, the bulk of the keywords has remained the same for some time. For the most part, the time spent manually defining the keywords for our environmental forces concepts was a one-time effort. (When we use the term "keywords," we mean "keywords and phrases." However, with few exceptions, we use keywords rather than phrases to identify concepts.)

Why Consider Text Mining?

Rapid examination of large amounts of text available in various text databases can give an organization a competitive edge. If an organization takes a hard look at historic industry-related trends, that organization might gain some knowledge of the industry future.

If there were correlations between major environmental forces in the past, those same correlations may exist in the future. If chart patterns derived from text appear to have predicted some past event, those same patterns might be used as indicators of future events.

Text that conforms to our text warehouse definition can be probed just as the data in data warehouses are probed. While text mining is a more difficult process than data mining, text mining is one of the best ways to isolate certain types of information. And while the examination of organization-internal databases is useful and can be quite fruitful, the examination of organization-external business information sources can also be useful and fruitful.

Being able to inspect information about competitors and other environmental forces, for example, can be especially valuable for drawing inferences about your present and future business environment. And it is ordinarily necessary to examine organization-external, rather than organization-internal, sources to obtain this kind of information.

In general, you will not learn by scanning your internal databases that a newly introduced technology can help your organization's productivity numbers. And, in general, you will not learn from an examination of your internal databases that a governmental regulation under review may negatively affect your organization's operations. You will most likely need to access and review organization-external information sources. Most of the information in these external sources will likely be in the form of unstructured text.

Environmental Forces and Text Mining

Learning to examine unstructured business text can help an organization create a competitive advantage. By using text mining methods on the business text, an organization can locate environmental opportunities and threats, giving the organization a better chance to understand the present. And by using business indicators derived from the text mining experience, the organization may be able to set environmental triggers based on those indicators that notify the organization of possible future business events, before the events are widely recognized by competitors.

We show how text mining and visualization methods (techniques for representing data or text pictorially) can be used to examine text and identify useful business concepts. The analysis of these concepts can enable an organization to better navigate the forces at work in its industry and better understand a competitor's strategic capability and activities. The analysis of these concepts can enable an organization to determine what its next business move should be.

Secondary Information and Text Mining

A large part of business information is secondary information. Text mining, as applied in this book, operates on secondary information. Secondary information is information obtained from a source other than an original source of the information. Primary information is information obtained from an original source (Fuld 1994, 35). A high percentage of secondary information is in text form.

The process in text mining, then, is usually as follows: Obtain secondary information in computer readable form, screen and classify the information so that the information conforms to the domain specifications, and analyze the information, using tools similar to those used in data mining. Some human intervention is ordinarily necessary to complete the process.

Secondary information can be quite useful in the overall business intelligence process. Many books on business intelligence or competitive intelligence have at least one section on gathering secondary information. Most experts feel that primary information is more valuable than secondary information in the creation of business intelligence. And while we do not disagree with this, we do feel that the use of text mining methods can make computerized secondary information a lot more valuable than many people believe it to be. Text mining can help improve the discovery process and enable computerized text information to be turned into intelligence more rapidly.

More and more secondary information is finding its way into electronic form. Therefore, more electronic information management technology should be used to insure that electronic secondary information is used to its greatest advantage. We should be utilizing techniques that allow us to make the maximum use of the secondary sources on online systems. And text mining is one of the techniques that can help us realize this maximum use.

Information Extraction

Information extraction is a special form of text mining. It is essentially a technique for locating specified text. Information extraction is very focused, using pre-established words or phrases to identify predetermined concepts. A text structure is defined, and software is written to "recognize" the text structure in text. That text structure is assumed to contain the kind of information desired.

We use information extraction to make the problem of text mining more manageable. The use of information extraction methods can allow you to ignore unimportant text and concentrate on the text that can be converted into business intelligence. Information extraction enables you to get to the meat of a key concept without wasting a lot of time reviewing irrelevant text. Being able to identify and extract concepts quickly can provide you with more time for confirming the secondary findings with primary research when necessary.

Some experts feel that using language patterns (phrases rather than keywords for example) as the information identification and extraction method is a more accurate way to identify and extract concepts. Concepts tend to be complex, the reasoning goes, therefore it takes language patterns, which are more complex than keywords, to identify concepts. While this may be generally true, we have found that using well-chosen keywords to identify information from an industry domain containing professionally written business news articles can often be an effective way to identify business concepts.

For example, the word "acquisition" in a business publication news article usually implies that some organization mentioned in the article is acquiring another organization. And the implied concept has something to do with two or more organizations entering into some type of business relationship. A reference to the word "market" or one of its derivatives in a business news article normally means that marketing activities, market size, the marketplace, or some other market related concept is being discussed. The implied concept has something to do with one or more of the following: an adjustment of a product or service price, a change in the production of a product or service, a new direction in the promotion of a product or service, or some modification to a product or service. Hence, we believe that keywords can identify certain business-related concepts under certain circumstances.

For the analysis described in this book, we identified two major types of concepts. They were those associated with the key environmental forces and those associated with competitors' activities. We used in-house developed text mining software to identify and extract the text representing these concepts.

KEYWORD-EXCERPT

We use industry domain keyword-excerpts to identify business-related concepts in business articles. A keyword-excerpt is text which contains a maximum of eight lines of text and at least one of the types of keywords mentioned above. A keyword-excerpt consists of the first two lines of the article's headline or title (if more than one line exists in the headline or title), the date of the article, the source of the article, and four lines from the body of the article. The second line of the four lines contains the environmental force keyword and the text of that line. The first, third and fourth lines contain text to help you interpret the business-related concept. (In the future, we will refer to these four lines as the "body" of the keyword-excerpt.)

For example, "Administration" is the keyword identifying the keyword-excerpt below taken from a 1992 UPI article on the air bag systems industry. (This keyword-excerpt contains six lines of text since the headline contains only one line of text and the fourth line of the body of the keyword-excerpt is a blank line.)

SOURCE: UPI
DATE: October 7, 1992
HEADLINE: Regulators Investigate Airbag Injuries, Malfunctions

"The newspaper reported in May that more than 500 drivers had complained to the National Highway Traffic Safety Administration in the previous 2 years about injuries caused by airbags and about airbags that failed to open in accidents."

CONCEPT DEFINITION

We've been using the word "concept" in this book and at this point we would like to discuss the word and its use. In the text mining and knowledge discovery arena, the word "concept" often takes on a special meaning. The "concept" represents the kind of information that text mining software tries to identify. When information extraction is used as the text mining method, a recognizable text structure is often defined for the concept. Text mining software is then written to recognize the text structure. The keyword-excerpt is the text structure our software recognizes.

Therefore, environmental force-related ideas, environmental force-related issues, environmental force-related facts, environmental force-related opinions, environmental force-related rumors, and environmental force-related conjecture are embedded in and represented by keyword-excerpts. (In practice, the essence of an environmental force-related concept is usually captured by one sentence in the keyword-excerpt.)

The "UPI" keyword-excerpt mentioned in the last section represents an air bag systems industry concept. That concept is an air bag systems industry issue that affects organizations in the industry. The issue is as follows: Air bags may have injured motorists, and the government is investigating the injuries. In our text mining process, the software automatically extracted the concept (in the form of a keyword-excerpt), and the software classified the concept with respect to its environmental force type. We then read and analyzed the concept to determine that the concept represented an air bag systems industry issue.

Chapter 1

SOFTWARE CONCEPT IDENTIFICATION AND EXTRACTION

Our in-house software contains a set of if-then rules that first identify force keywords. The software then identifies and extracts the keyword-excerpts. For example, the above "UPI" keyword-excerpt was identified with an if-then rule which selects all keyword-excerpts containing the keyword "Administration." All keyword-excerpts associated with a keyword from one of the ten key force types are written to computer files. The "UPI" keyword-excerpt above, which represents a government related concept, was written to a file and later read for meaning. We analyze concepts in the form of keyword-excerpts, individually, by reading the concepts, and as groups by using visualization methods.

VISUALIZATION

Visualization (which generally means putting the information into some pictorial form) is sometimes included as one of the tools of data mining. Visualization is a tool employed by data miners to elucidate trends or patterns in data. Scatter diagrams, pie charts, and line charts are among the pictorial forms sometimes used.

We use visualization to display in chart form certain text mining results—keywords and phrases—pertaining to environmental forces. The charts are the very simple kind—line and pie charts. For a calendar year, the pie charts are used to show the environmental force distributions, and the line charts are used to show the environmental force trends.

ONLINE SYSTEMS

Some online systems allow you to retrieve text that can be used in text mining. These systems have the appropriate content, stored in organized databases, that is needed for text analysis. And these systems offer high-caliber search engines necessary for well-defined content searching.

These systems include LexisNexis, Dialog and Factiva. The Internet commonly provides access to these systems. Online systems such as these have historical text that goes back well over ten years. These systems' content satisfies the above description of a text database.

LexisNexis, Dialog and Factiva allow researchers to search specific fields (or segments) of their databases. For example, in most of these systems' records, you can search the headlines (or titles) only, you can search the lead paragraphs only, you can search the lead paragraphs and the headlines only, or you can search some other field. These online systems provide many search-refinement features that permit precision searching. All three of the above-mentioned systems allow Boolean searches (using AND, NOT, OR in the search statements), and the use of proximity operators.

These operators allow you to further control the type of articles selected by the search engine based on keyword position within the text. At least two of the systems allow natural language searching. And, for the most part, when using any one of these systems' search engines, all records selected for search within the online system's database are searched equally. That is, with few exceptions, you do not need to worry that your search statement will "search" differently in different sections of one of these systems' databases.

These online systems also have various output options for displaying text from sources that meet the search statement criteria. For example, you can output the lead paragraph plus the bibliographic citation and the word count without outputting the full text of the article. In many cases, you can output the title only. And there are other output options available.

Using these systems' and similar systems' search and output capabilities, and additional text analysis or text mining software tools, a user can retrieve and screen text from articles that conform to a set of domain requirements.

Internet Websites also provide access to useful textual information. Although much of this information is not stored in an organized database, you can access a great deal of the information using an Internet search engine. Two of the best-known Internet search engines are Yahoo and Google—Google being the most popular.

Online Systems' Content

Wire services, magazines, newsletters, and other business news sources can provide an accurate reflection of the distribution of U.S. business environmental forces for some industries. (An environmental force is an external event that can cause your organization to achieve or fail to achieve a business objective or business goal. These forces include technology forces, governmental forces, political forces, and the other forces mentioned above.) An accurate reflection can be provided for the entire U.S. if enough relevant text is extracted from an appropriate number of well-distributed U.S. news sources.

In our experience, reviewing at least one hundred news sources well-distributed across the fifty states gives you a good chance of capturing the key prevailing explanations, opinions, actions, and expectations of business writers, key business leaders, political groups, the government, and other business players associated with an organization's external environment. Therefore, this type of review gives you a good chance of capturing the key industry-related forces. The more relevant the obtained text, the higher the probability that the correct trends, distributions, and competitor activities will be captured. We show results that address our assertion below.

Using an Online System for Trend, Distribution, and Competitor Analysis

To test our assertion that reviewing a representative collection of news sources can give you an accurate reflection of key industry-related forces, we selected two industries for investigation. One of the industries was the satellite industry (some organizations in this industry launch telecommunications satellites, for example), as defined by the following Dun & Bradstreet (D&B) standard industrial classification (SIC) codes: 4899-9905, 4841-9905, 3663-9909, and 3663-9910. The other industry was the personal computer industry, as defined by the following D&B SIC code: 3571-9904.

An industry is defined by the set of organizations in the industry. Therefore, we decided to determine how many industry organizations found in the D&B database, implied above, could also be found in a set of articles from an online system's database containing a representative collection of business news sources. We first retrieved the names of publicly held organizations in our two industries from the D&B database. We then retrieved a set of articles related to these two industries from the online system's database articles.

We created a D&B list of our industry-related organizations. And on comparing the organization names on the D&B list with organization names from the online system's articles, we found that over 75 percent of the organizations on the D&B list were in the articles retrieved from the online system's database. We read many of the articles and determined that the articles did give us an accurate understanding of each industry's competitors (especially the leading competitors).

To look at the distribution of key environmental forces, we investigated the key forces of two sub-industries of the two industries mentioned above. The first sub-industry was the commercial satellite industry (which would not include, for example, federal government related organizations that put up satellites for scientific research).

The second sub-industry was the personal computer appliance industry which is a subset of the personal computer industry. Organizations that make handheld units such as Personal Digital Assistants or PDAs, for example, are in this industry.

Based on our industry knowledge, we felt that "government" was the dominant force (the number of associated concepts was the largest) in the commercial satellite industry during the 1980s. And we felt that "technology" was the dominant force in the personal computer industry during the 1990s. To test these feelings, we first retrieved industry-related articles from our selected online system. We then scanned the business articles and extracted concepts for the two industries using our text mining software. Finally, we created pie and trend charts for the ten force types described above.

In figure 1.1, you can see that the government was the dominant force in the 1989 commercial satellite industry. And in figure 1.2, you can see that technology was the dominant force in the 1998 personal computer appliance industry. The underlying trends for the two industries are shown in figures 1.3 and 1.4. Although we didn't try to predict what the trends would look like for these industries, we did expect the dominant force's trend pattern to contain most of the "highest-peaks" during a year. And this occurred in both the commercial satellite and the personal computer appliance industries.

Our results don't prove that all key forces exhibited the correct distributions. However, we believe the dominant forces are correct, and the organization-related information is accurate. This is very important in our environmental analysis.

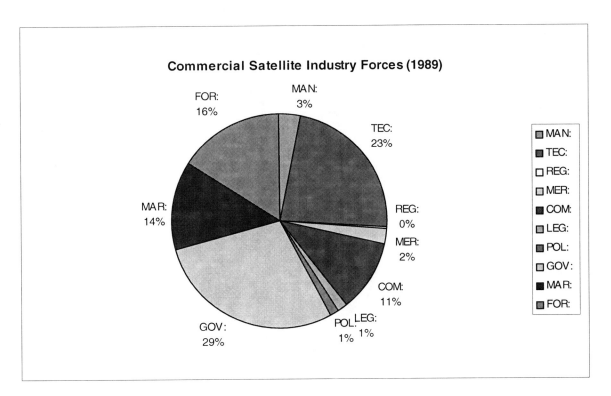

Fig. 1.1

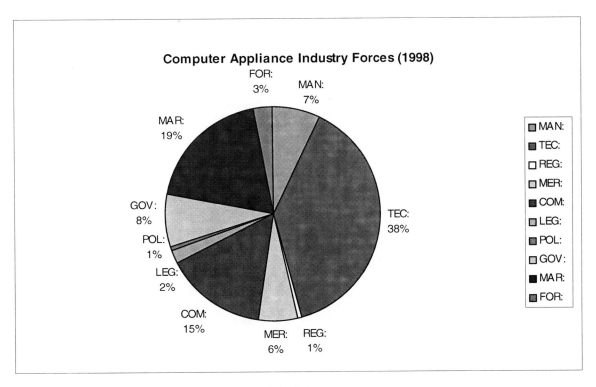

Fig. 1.2

Note: The above charts are associated with environmental force distributions.

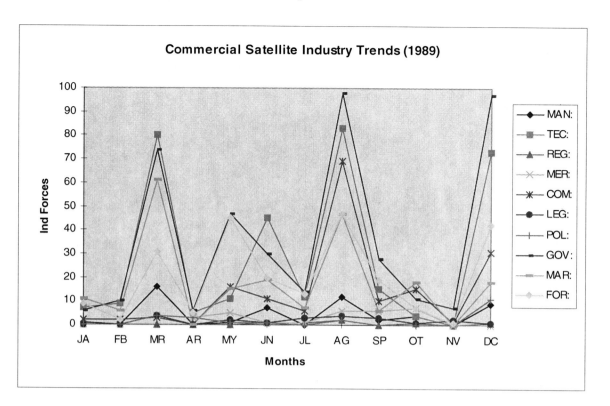

Fig. 1.3

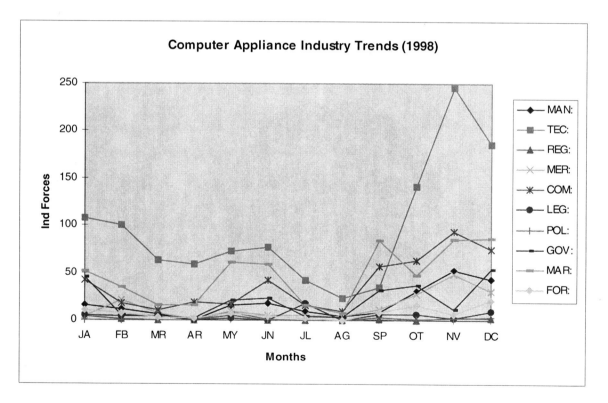

Fig. 1.4

Note: The above charts are associated with environmental force trends.

The Use of Online Systems

We retrieved text from the LexisNexis Regional News Library to create the results shown in the first edition of this book. When we created the results, the Regional News Library contained over twenty-five years of historical information associated with the air bag systems industry. And in the library, we could access a set of over 135 regional daily U.S. newspapers. Wire services and other sources of news were also included in the library. This library contained newspapers from all but five states (Vermont, Mississippi, Hawaii, South Dakota, and Montana, as of September 1999). As of February 1, 1999, there were 1,489 daily newspapers published in the United States (Maddux 1999, vii). So the set of more than 135 regional daily newspapers in the Regional News Library represented about 9 percent of the total daily newspapers in the U.S.

Nine percent may be viewed as a relatively small sample by some. And indeed, ordinarily in statistical analysis, the larger the sample the more accurate the results. However, in practice it has been found that a relatively small sample can be used with confidence if the small sample accurately represents the characteristics of the total population. For example, in the U.S., less than two thousand people are generally polled by major polling organizations to predict the outcome of a presidential election. But the results are typically found to be good predictors of the winner and loser of the election when the population sample accurately represents the opinions of the voting population (Oskamp 1999).

Based on the analysis described above, and the percentage and distribution of U.S. newspapers represented in the Regional News Library, we felt that we could confidently use text from the news library for trend, distribution, and competitor analysis. Therefore, we used text from the news library for the air bag industry analysis presented in the first edition of this book. Since we still have confidence in that industry text, we decided we didn't need to retrieve new text for the air bag analysis discussed in this revised edition.

EXAMINING THE BARIATRIC INDUSTRY USING OUR METHODS

As we mentioned earlier, we are now applying our methods to the health care industry. In particular, we are applying our methods to the bariatric or weight loss segment of that industry. We view this segment as a sub-industry of the health care industry, and we will refer to this segment as the bariatric or weight loss industry. Now, we want to present an example of a force distribution chart associated with this industry, and an example of a force trend chart associated with this industry.

We said, above, that most of the results shown in this book were created using text from the LexisNexis Regional News Library. However, over the past few years we have also used text from Factiva in our text mining analysis. In fact, the bariatric industry-related charts shown in this section were generated using Factiva text—specifically, 2007 business text.

As you can see in figure 1.5 below, technology was the dominant force in the bariatric or weight loss industry for 2007. Marketing was the second most dominant force. And the government was the third most dominant force for that year. We think that it is reasonable that technology would be dominant. As we indicated earlier, "research" is a keyword in our technology category. And research is important to the bariatric industry.

Today, the obesity and overweight issues represent a pressing worldwide health problem. And a lot of research is being devoted to finding ways to combat the problem. Because research is so necessary in developing new technology to solve the problem, there is an abundance of research-related concepts helping to drive the technology force.

There is research directed at weight loss medications, research aimed at weight loss and weight management exercise and diet programs, and ongoing research into bariatric or weight loss surgical procedures. Hence, since research is a component of our technology force, we would expect technology to reflect the profusion of weight loss research. And we would expect technology to garner a large portion of the force distribution chart.

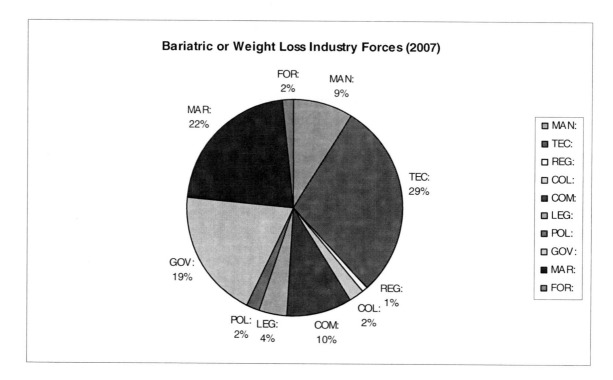

Fig. 1.5

Note: The above chart is associated with environmental force distributions

The technology trend shown in figure 1.6, below, gives added evidence that technology was indeed dominant for most of the months during 2007. The chart also highlights those months where the market and government forces prevailed during the year.

Without a doubt, a prudent strategic manager working in the weight loss or bariatric industry could use distribution and trend information to determine a likely future focus of the industry. For example, the manager could gain knowledge of a potentially significant, future weight loss medication by analyzing the concepts used to create the "research" portions of the bariatric distribution and trend charts.

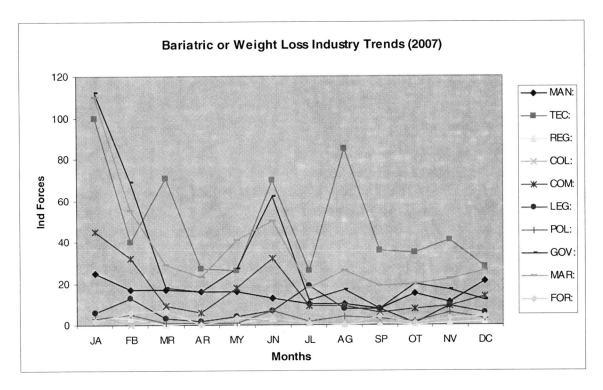

Fig. 1.6

Note: The above chart is associated with environmental force trends.

SOME CLARIFICATION

At this point, we should clarify something concerning the above-mentioned online systems' content. We do not believe that the online systems' sources used for this book's analysis are the only sources of useful business information.

We believe that other online sources such as organization Websites, Internet newsgroups, listservs, forums, blogs and social network sites, can be important business information sources. Any of these sources could serve as gateways to relevant government studies, regulations, litigation, or new technology. And there may be times when someone will reveal useful information about one of your competitors in a forum, newsgroup, listserv, or blog.

Also as we indicated above, we believe that primary information is generally superior to secondary information. More times than not, primary information can be more helpful and timely than secondary information. In a discussion, for instance, an industry expert may provide insight based on gut instinct that surpasses any information obtained from any secondary source.

Nevertheless, we do believe that online secondary textual information can be more useful if automated techniques are employed to examine the increasing amount of business-related online text. Indeed, we believe that this organization-external online business-related text can be "mined" proficiently for distribution, trend, and competitor information. We believe that this mining activity can be an important component of an organization's strategic planning.

PULLING IT TOGETHER

Environmental forces are events that can cause an organization to achieve or fail to achieve its business objectives. Environmental forces include the actions, opinions, and expectations of key players in an industry's environment. Many times the environmental forces for various industries are revealed in text found on organization-external online systems.

We can obtain an accurate representation of business environmental forces, including competitor activities within the U.S., if we extract enough concepts (at least 500) from articles that satisfy the following criteria:

- The concepts come from at least one hundred articles containing relevant domain text.

- Each article in the domain text contains at least one complete sentence.

- Each article contains at least one instance of an industry-defining word or phrase.

- Each article has a time stamp.

- The articles in the domain text are taken from news sources from the northern, southern, eastern and western regions of the U.S.

- All articles were published within the same time period. (We feel that a reasonable period is one year or less.)

If the above criteria are met (or almost met), it is highly probable that relevant concepts can be identified and extracted. These concepts can then be counted, compared, and charted. By using specially designed software, most of the counting, comparing, and charting can be completed in less time than it would take to perform the tasks by hand. And you can obtain results that provide an accurate representation of industry-related trends, distribution, and competitor activities.

We would like to emphasize that even if all elements of the criteria are not met, the results may still be accurate. However, how accurate you take the results to be depends on other analyses you've done, and the conclusions you drew from those analyses.

Overview of Our Text Mining Process and Our Text Mining Software

We wrote the text mining software used to create many of the results in this book in the BASIC software language. That software controls most of the text mining process discussed above.

The software first screens each article retrieved from an online system. The screening is done to determine if an article indeed contains one of the industry-defining words or phrases. Sometimes an online system's search engine may select articles that correctly satisfy the search statement, but do not satisfy the industry domain's criteria. For example, consider the following text: "We breathe air, bags hold groceries . . ." Some search engines will see "air, bags" as "air bags," since some engines don't see commas. Therefore, a non-air bag systems article containing the words ". . . air, bag . . ." could be selected by a search engine as an air bag systems industry article even though the article could be irrelevant to the air bag systems industry.

So our in-house software identifies and excludes non-domain articles to prevent the corruption of the domain articles. After it excludes non-domain articles, the software screens the remaining articles for relevant business keywords and phrases. The software identifies and extracts these relevant keywords and phrases using if-then rules described above. The software then writes the keywords and phrases to computer files. The software also writes to files the associated concepts (keyword-excerpts), including competitor-related concepts (discussed in chapter 3). The software classifies and counts keywords and phrases which identified the concepts. Associated information is written to files. The keywords and phrases are then subjected to visualization or charting tools (illustrated in chapter 2) and competitor-related if-then rules (discussed in chapter 3).

We show our text mining and business analysis process flow in figure 1.7. Except for the "pasting" of tabular data into a spreadsheet that is designed to automatically create charts, every process component within the "bracket" on the process flow is automated with our in-house software. As indicated, it usually takes less than one hour to complete the process for a year's worth of an industry's domain-related text.

The process flow shows that the analysis of the distribution charts, trend charts, and the concepts represented by the keyword-excerpts, has to be done manually to find opportunities and threats. The advantage of using the text mining process as outlined is that the software reduces the time it takes to find relevant text for opportunity and threat analysis. The actual amount of time necessary to complete the analysis, however, is a function of your industry knowledge and analytical skills.

Text Mining Software

The software used for the text mining in this book is not for sale. But there are organizations producing commercial text mining or text analysis software. One such organization is IBM. Another is SPSS Inc. If you are interested in learning more about the capabilities of these organizations' software offerings, please contact the organizations.

Text Mining and Business Analysis Process Flow

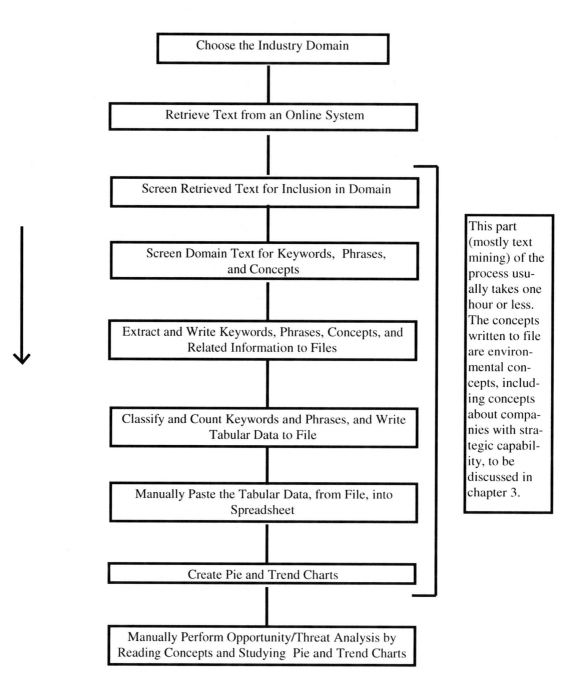

Fig. 1.7

Effectiveness and Efficiency of Our Text Mining Process

An important feature of our text mining process is that it presents you with relevant, but less text than is usual to read, thus reducing analysis time. To illustrate the reduction in text associated with our process, we created a set of comparison tables.

Tables 1.1, 1.2, and 1.3 below show comparisons between different compositions of air bag systems industry text. This text was generated for the 1989-through-1998 period. All text was either retrieved from online, or extracted from the retrieved text (in the form of keyword-excerpts) by the in-house software described above. In two of the following tables we show how focusing just on the concepts (keyword-excerpts) identified in and extracted from the retrieved text, rather than on all the retrieved text, decreases the amount of text that has to be reviewed (tables 1.2 and 1.3).

Table 1.1 presents a general description of the text that was retrieved and mined. For example, 129 articles were retrieved for 1989. Two hundred and seven pages were in that text. The dominant force (the force with the most concepts and whose keywords were mentioned most often) for 1989 was "government."

We have found that a good way to reduce the number of concepts for review is to analyze concepts associated with the most-frequently-mentioned keyword from the dominant force's class of keywords. The most-frequently-mentioned keyword for 1989 in the class of governmental keywords was "federal." This keyword is indicated on the second column and last row of table 1.1.

Text-composition information is shown for each of the ten years, allowing you to compare the amount of text retrieved, the dominant force, and the most-frequently-mentioned keyword for each of the ten years. (Note that there was a general increase in the amount of air bag systems industry text retrieved from 1989 to 1998.)

Table 1.1
Description of Air Bag Systems Text for 1989–1998

Year of Text	1989	1990	1991	1992	1993	1994	1995	1996	1997	1998
Total No. Articles in Text	129	145	111	83	187	239	379	1050	1308	795
Total Pages in Retrieved Text	207	423	264	252	561	678	528	1665	1976	1231
Dominant Force	government	government	government	government	technology	technology	government	government	government	government
Dominant Force Most-Freq Keyword	federal	federal	admin	admin	design	technology	agenc	government	government	government

Chapter 1

We extracted concepts for each year of the ten-year period. Table 1.2 compares the total pages of text retrieved from the online system for one year to the total pages of text associated with all concepts extracted from the retrieved text by our software for that year. In 1989, for example, there were 207 pages of air bag systems industry text retrieved from online, while there were 152 pages of text extracted for the industry concepts. Therefore, the text associated with the concepts is 73 percent of the total text retrieved for the 1989 air bag systems industry, as shown on the last row of table 1.2.

This means that if you read only the 1989 concepts you could reduce the amount of reading material necessary to determine likely 1989 environmental opportunities and threats by 27 percent (100 percent minus 73 percent). The percentages for concept pages for each year are shown on the last row of table 1.2.

Table 1.2
Comparison of Total-Pages-in-Text to Total-Pages-in-Concept-Text for 1989–1998

Year of Text	1989	1990	1991	1992	1993	1994	1995	1996	1997	1998
Total Pages in Retrieved Text	207	423	264	252	561	678	528	1665	1976	1231
Total Pages in Concept (Key-word-Excerpt) Text	152	132	96	94	160	226	341	1382	1578	986
Percentage of Pages in Concept (Keyword-Excerpt) Text	73%	31%	36%	37%	29%	33%	65%	83%	80%	80%

As we've said, our concepts take the form of a keyword-excerpt, and keyword-excerpts are identified with one of our force-type keywords. As indicated above, focusing on relevant text is important. To home in on relevant concepts, our software extracts and collects the keyword-excerpts representing the concepts identified by the most-frequently-mentioned keyword associated with a year's dominant force. Thus, if the government force was the dominant force, and "federal" was the most-frequently-mentioned government force-type keyword, all concepts identified by "federal" would have been collected and made available by the software.

Table 1.3 below compares the total pages of text retrieved for a year to the total pages associated with concepts for the dominant force's most-frequently-mentioned keyword. (The total number of pages associated with the most-frequently-mentioned keyword concepts are shown on the third row of table 1.3.)

For example, if you read only the concepts associated with the dominant force's most-frequently-mentioned keyword, you would read only 10 percent of the 1989 text (see the last row of table 1.3). And you could evaluate likely opportunities and threats associated with the dominant force. Indeed, in no year would you have to read more than 14 percent of the text to obtain a year's worth of information about a dominant force. We demonstrate the use of this technique in chapter 2.

Table 1.3
Comparison of Total-Pages-in-Text for 1989–1998 to Total-Pages-in-Concepts
(for Most-Frequent Keyword)

Year of Text	1989	1990	1991	1992	1993	1994	1995	1996	1997	1998
Total Pages in Retrieved Text	207	423	264	252	561	678	528	1665	1976	1231
Total Pages in Concepts (Keyword-Excerpts) for Most-Freq Keyword	21	19	14	13	29	24	39	218	283	146
Percentage of Pages in Concepts (Keyword-Excerpts) for Most-Freq Keyword Text	10%	4%	5%	5%	5%	4%	7%	13%	14%	12%

Chapter 1

SUMMARY

Business intelligence can involve a broad array of ideas and opinions. Business intelligence can mean anything and everything having to do with using business information. The intelligence might include knowledge of the present and some very educated guesses about the future. For us, business intelligence is any information that reveals opportunities and threats that motivate an organization to take some action. We believe that business intelligence is at the heart of strategic management.

We introduce text mining as a way to scan and examine organization-external business text to gain business intelligence. Text mining is the process of identifying concepts in, and extracting concepts from, large amounts of unstructured text in computerized databases using methods that permit further analysis of the concepts. The use of text mining and effective analysis methods can make business intelligence more accessible.

We will show you the results of applying text mining methods to a real industry. That industry is the air bag systems industry. Once text mining has made the business information available, we will use information analysis techniques to convert the information into actions beneficial to our fictional organization, **Mythical Air Bag Materials**.

One of our first areas of focus is that of external environmental forces. These forces include technology forces, political forces, governmental forces, and other forces. We will analyze these forces to determine how they might affect an organization. We will perform much of the analysis using visualization methods.

Our second area of focus is that of competitor forces. Although competitor forces are part of the environmental forces, we give special attention to competitor forces. We do this because competitor activities exert some of the strongest forces within an industry.

Environmental forces are identified as "concepts." Concepts include ideas, issues, facts, opinions, rumors, and conjecture. Concepts are represented by keyword-excerpts (a maximum of eight lines of text containing a keyword). Concepts, in the form of keyword-excerpts, are identified and extracted from text using text mining techniques. The text mining techniques are information extraction methods whereby only the concepts of interest are identified and extracted. We analyze the concepts to find opportunities and threats for our organization, **Mythical Air Bag Materials**.

Chapter 2   Environmental Forces Analysis

CHAPTER OVERVIEW

This chapter focuses on air bag systems environmental forces concepts. The concepts take the form of keyword-excerpts defined in chapter 1. Our text mining software extracts and writes the keyword-excerpts to computer files for visualization and strategic analysis. Below is an example of a governmental force keyword-excerpt or concept. "Federal" is the keyword that identified the concept.

SOURCE: The Record
DATE: July 29, 1990
HEADLINE: Air-Bag Rupture Report in Hudson Is Probed

"One federal agency has concluded that an automotive air-safety bag did not rupture during a July 14 accident in Union City, while a second federal agency is still investigating."

Keywords and phrases associated with the environmental concepts, like the one above, are first analyzed as forces using visualization techniques. Individual concepts, identified by the keywords and phrases, are then analyzed. The ultimate goal of both the visualization analysis and the individual concept analysis is to find opportunities and threats. Strategic comments, which describe opportunities and threats associated with the concepts, are shown to indicate how our organization, **Mythical Air Bag Materials**, should manage the existing environmental conditions.

Chapter 2

THE AIR BAG SYSTEMS INDUSTRY

Structurally, the air bag systems industry is defined by five types of organizations associated with air bag systems products or services. These five types of organizations are as follows: direct rivals to an organization in the air bag systems industry, buyers of products and services in the air bag systems industry, suppliers of products and services in the air bag systems industry, organizations providing substitutes for products or services offered by organizations in the air bag systems industry, and potential entrants to the air bag systems industry.

Textually, the air bag systems industry domain is defined by articles that contain the following words or phrases: airbag, airbags, air-bag, air-bags, air bag, or air bags. This method for characterizing the industry domain text was discussed in chapter 1.

Chapter 2 is about analysis. To involve you in the analytical process, we ask you to pretend that you work for **Mythical Air Bag Materials** as a strategic analyst and that your organization's direct rival is another air bag fabric maker.

On the pages that follow, you will find an analysis of the air bag systems industry for each year of the ten-year period 1989–1998. The 1989–1998 period was chosen because the federal government mandated the use of passive restraint systems in all new automobiles during the beginning of this period. The mandate played a significant role in heightening the interest in air bag systems. Thus, analyzing a ten-year period for the industry starting with 1989 is appropriate.

We believe that, if possible, five, ten, or even fifteen-year periods of historical industry-related text should be analyzed to understand an industry. Planning for the long-term future can be enhanced by analyzing the long-term past. Text mining can deliver the information to make this analysis practical.

We discuss environmental forces for 1989 through 1998. We analyze distribution charts, trend charts, and extracted concepts associated with these forces. Although we show charts based on all concepts, we don't have the space to show all of the concepts. Therefore, for the extracted concept analysis in this book, we only consider the December concepts associated with the dominant environmental force. Further, we only consider December concepts associated with the most-frequently-mentioned dominant force keyword.

We have found that one sentence usually captures the essence of a concept, even if the identifying keyword is not in the sentence. Therefore, for our concept analysis, we analyze one sentence and headline from each of the December concepts (keyword-excerpts representing the concepts) for the most-frequently-mentioned dominant force keyword. For each set of December concepts, we indicate the most-frequently-mentioned keyword that identified the concepts.

These concepts are subsets of the full year's concepts whose keywords were used to create the charts. For each chart, we perform an analysis to locate patterns that may be useful for strategic planning, and we review each concept to identify the concept's opportunity and threat relevance. (While only the December concepts are shown, we analyzed more of the year's concepts to get a feel for the underlying causes of a chart distribution or trend.)

Chapter 2·

Using our text mining software, we examined over 4,000 air bag systems industry domain articles to produce the charts and concepts shown on the following pages. Less than 10 percent of the articles from which concepts and charts were generated received any manual skimming for additional information or text. In the concept analysis shown on the following pages where we manually extracted additional text, we indicate this with a note.

Text mining reduced much of the manual effort. As you will see, the resulting charts and concepts do provide useful insights into opportunities and threats. We should note that the analysis for each of the ten years is assumed to be taking place during the last day of December of the associated year. We also assume that our organization, **Mythical Air Bag Materials**, is performing the analysis in real-time. So, for example when we perform the 1989 environmental forces analysis, we do not yet have the 1990 forces text. It will be one year before we will have the text to perform the 1990 analysis. By the time we perform the 1990 analysis, our organization will have completed its analysis for 1989, and those analysis results will be on file.

AIR BAG SYSTEMS INDUSTRY FORCES ANALYSIS FOR 1989
(We will use "industry forces" to mean "environmental forces.")

1989 Pie and Trend Chart Analysis

We examined 129 articles identifying 944 concepts for the 1989 air bag systems industry analysis. Figures 2.1 and 2.2 on the following page show pie and trend charts. These charts indicate that the government was the dominant force for 1989, although at times during the year, technology was dominant. It makes sense that the government was dominant. The government mandated that all new cars in the United States have passive restraint systems for front seat passengers, such as air bags or automatic seat belts, starting in the early 1990s. So the government (in the form of the National Highway Traffic Safety Administration in some cases) was more or less driving the air bag systems industry.

Technology was the second most dominant force. The competitor force (COM) was in third place. The trend chart shows how the forces interacted throughout the year. Government and technology forces dominated most of the months of the year. There were two months when competitor forces were dominant.

It would appear that **Mythical Air Bag Materials** should monitor the government's activities and try to take advantage of any forthcoming regulations. In general, political forces (POL) drive governmental forces (GOV), which drive regulatory (REG) forces. More opportunities may be around the corner for **Mythical Air Bag Materials**.

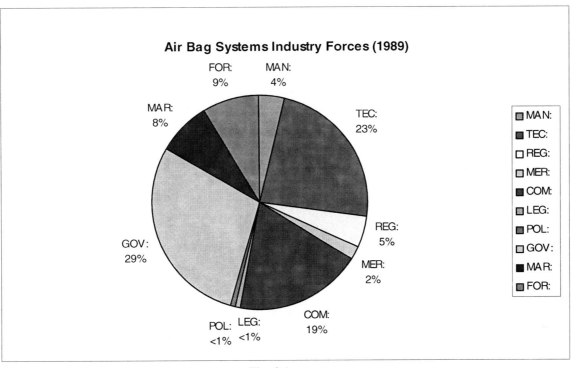

Fig. 2.1

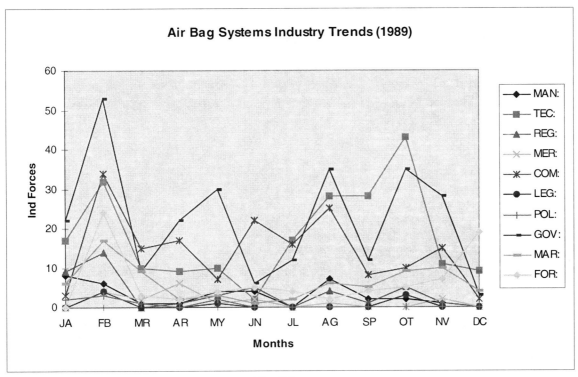

Fig. 2.2

Note: The above distribution and trend charts are associated with the 1989 environmental forces.

Environmental Forces Analysis

1989 Extracted Concept Analysis

Below we show concepts and strategic comments for the air bag systems industry for December of 1989. Dominant force concepts are shown for the most-frequently-mentioned keyword. The dominant force for 1989 was government. The most-frequently-mentioned keyword was "federal." Therefore, the concepts below were identified by the keyword "federal."

The concepts support the force charts in that they tell us what activities are really behind the charts. The concepts also give us some idea of what specific opportunities and threats exist within our business environment.

Dominant Environmental Force Concepts

1989 Concept 1

Source: Chicago Tribune
Date: December 10, 1989
Headline: Carmakers Play It Safe for '90s: Passive Restraints a Start

Concept Sentence: "The safety issue, however, is one that also now is being mandated by federal law; manufacturers must equip cars with passive restraints - belts, air bags or other items that don't require such action as buckling a belt."

Strategic Comment: We see this as an opportunity for our organization, **Mythical Air Bag Materials,** since air bags are one of the main passive restraint systems, and we make air bag fabric.

1989 Concept 2

Source: The San Diego Union-Tribune
Date: December 2, 1989
Headline: Chrysler Looks into Complaints of Air-Bag Burns

Concept Sentence: "Chrysler first learned of the problems in September, when passive restraints became mandatory in U.S. cars, said Al Slechter, federal technical affairs director for the automaker."

Strategic Comment: Air bag burns could be a threat for our organization. We need to determine what role the fabric plays in the burns associated with air bags.

Chapter 2

AIR BAG SYSTEMS INDUSTRY FORCES ANALYSIS FOR 1990

1990 Pie and Trend Chart Analysis

The next two charts, figures 2.3 and 2.4, address the air bag systems industry for 1990. We examined 145 articles identifying 824 concepts. From the pie chart (figure 2.3), we can see that the governmental force continued to be the dominant force for 1990. Technology moved to third place in 1990 from its 1989 second-place status, while the competitor force moved to second place in 1990. We should note that the governmental force had a larger piece of the total pie in 1990 than it did in 1989. Again, this emphasizes the strong role that government has played in the air bag systems industry.

Looking at the trend chart (figure 2.4), the market force appears to be somewhat correlated with the competitor force. From 1989 to 1990, as indicated above, there was a relative increase in governmental activity. The government was a positive influence on the air bag systems industry. And there appears to be some correlation between governmental activity and competitor activity (figure 2.4).

Again, looking at the trend chart, there is an obvious gap near the latter part of the year between the government, technology, and competitor forces, and the rest of the ten environmental force types. We can surmise that competitors were responding to the government's passive restraint mandate by trying to improve the air bag systems technology. **Mythical Air Bag Materials** should seek out the technological leaders and determine if any competitor is producing a superior fabric to ours. A superior fabric produced by a competitor would indeed be a threat to our organization.

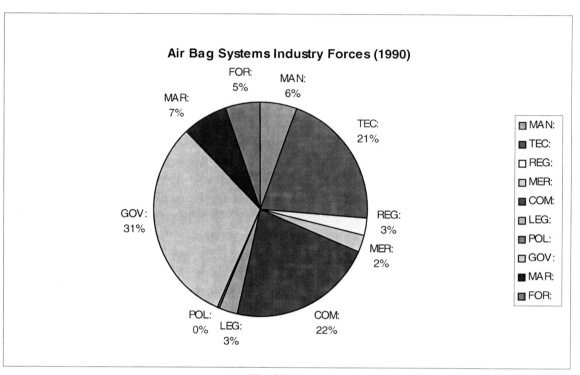

Fig. 2.3

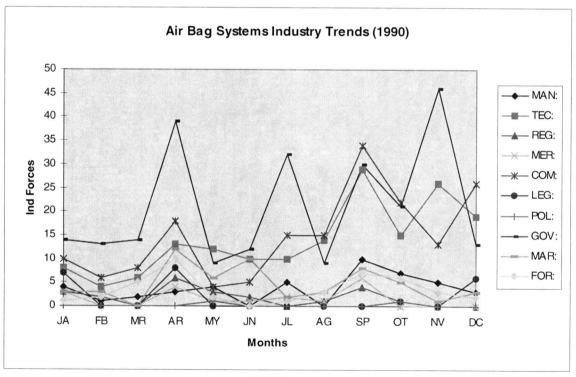

Fig. 2.4

Note: The above distribution and trend charts are associated with the 1990 environmental forces.

Chapter 2

1990 Extracted Concept Analysis

Below we show concepts from 1990 that support the above pie and trend charts. We present dominant force December concepts for the most-frequently-mentioned keyword. The dominant force for 1990 was government. The most-frequently-mentioned government keyword was "federal." Therefore, the concepts below were identified by the keyword "federal."

The concepts below show that there was talk of air bag recalls. The recalls represent a threat to our industry.

Dominant Environmental Force Concepts

1990 Concept 1

Source: Chicago Tribune
Date: December 30, 1990
Headline: Air-Bag Recalls Are Expanding

Concept Sentence: "Air bags or some other driver-side passive-restraint system, such as automatic safety belts, have been federally mandated for all domestically sold cars beginning with the 1990 model year."

Strategic Comment: While the federal mandate continues to present an opportunity for our organization, the fact that some air bags are being recalled presents a threat. We need to collaborate with the leading makers of air bag systems in our industry. We should also determine if the recalls are in any way associated with air bag fabric.

1990 Concept 2

Source: Newsday
Date: December 26, 1990
Headline: Product Recalls:
               From Faulty Auto Air Bags to Greasy Medical Tools

Concept Sentence: "THESE PRODUCT RECALLS were announced recently by the federal government and, in some cases, the organizations involved."

Strategic Comment: We need to determine why air bags were recalled. We need to determine what the problems are. Air bag system recalls present a possible threat to our organization.

1990 Concept 3

Source: Los Angeles Times
Date: December 18, 1990
Headline: Chrysler to Offer Air Bags on Its Minivans in Early '91

Concept Sentence: "The federal government, which requires automatic seat belts or air bags in cars being made today, will require passive restraint systems in light trucks by the 1995 model year."

Strategic Comment: This concept indicates what could present an opportunity for us. We need to contact the air bag systems suppliers and offer to collaborate with them. We should determine if there are suppliers that specialize in the truck area. If so, we can make sure that we conform to whatever their special requirements might be.

Chapter 2

AIR BAG SYSTEMS INDUSTRY FORCES ANALYSIS FOR 1991

1991 Pie and Trend Chart Analysis

For 1991, we examined 111 articles, identifying 526 relevant concepts. From the pie chart, we can see that the governmental force was continuing to be the dominant force (figure 2.5). By 1991, all new U.S. cars had passive restraint systems, and the government was more concerned about motorists' air bag-related complaints.

While the competitor force was the second most dominant force for 1990, we see that technology came back as the second most dominant force for 1991 (figure 2.5). Although the marketing force has been almost constant for three years, it appears to rise and fall, to some extent, with the competitor forces during a year.

Reviewing the trend chart (figure 2.6), we can see that although the government was the dominant force most of the year, there was a somewhat downward trend in its dominance during 1991. And again, there appears to be a loose correlation between the competitor and marketing forces, reflecting, perhaps, that much of the competitor activity was in the marketing area.

The government aided in the creation of a marketing opportunity when it pushed air bags, and this works to our benefit. We should review our competitor's marketing material and continue to monitor the government's activities.

41

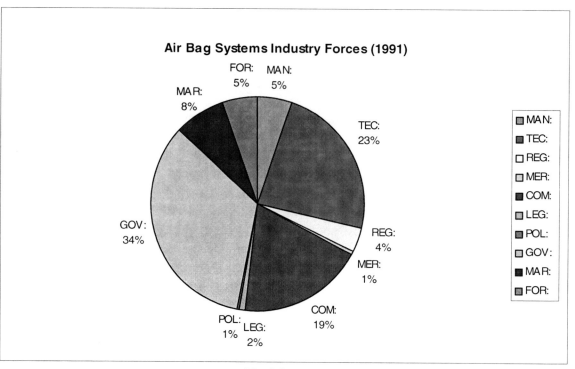

Fig. 2.5

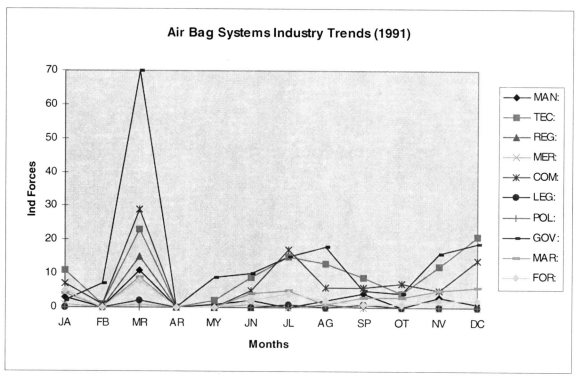

Fig. 2.6

Note: The above distribution and trend charts are associated with the 1991 environmental forces.

Chapter 2

1991 Extracted Concept Analysis

Below we show December concepts from the 1991 articles which support the pie and trend charts. Dominant force concepts are shown for the most-frequently-mentioned keyword. The dominant force for 1991 was government. The most-frequently-mentioned government keyword was "admin" (as in "administration"). Therefore, the concepts below were identified by the keyword "admin." ("Admin" is actually a keyword root. We will refer to keyword roots as keywords.)

The following concepts address air bag-related dangers to children, and there is also more talk about GM's air bag installation plans.

Dominant Environmental Force Concepts

1991 Concept 1

Source: The Atlanta Journal and Constitution
Date: December 13, 1991
Headline: GM Moves up Plans, Will Install Two Air Bags in '98
Vans and Light Trucks

Concept Sentence: "The National Highway Traffic Safety Administration is mandating that all light trucks and vans sold in the United States have passive restraints - either air bags or automatic shoulder belts."

Strategic Comment: The government is mandating passive restraint systems for light trucks and vans sold in the United States for 1995 to 1998 model years. This concept continues to confirm that there are opportunities for us in the air bag systems industry.

1991 Concept 2

Source: Chicago Tribune
Date: December 11, 1991
Headline: Infant Car Seat, Air Bag Could Be Dangerous Mix

Concept Sentence: "Jerry Ralph Curry, head of the National Highway Traffic Safety Administration, said a child placed in such a seat could be seriously injured if the air bag deploys."

43

Strategic Comment: There is danger associated with placing a child in a child seat where he or she could be subjected to the force of an air bag deployment. This danger represents a threat for those in the air bag industry. We should determine if there is anything we can do at our organization to minimize the dangers associated with air bag inflation.

1991 Concept 3

Source: U.P.I.
Date: December 3, 1991
Headline: GM to Put Air Bags in All Light Trucks, Vans

Concept Sentence: "GM's air bag plans, Reuss said, reflected a decision by the company to meet the National Highway Traffic Safety Administration's (NHTSA) passive restraint standard for light trucks and vans with air bags rather than automatic safety belts."

Strategic Comment: GM is planning to install air bags rather than automatic seat belts. This presents an opportunity for our organization. Since GM is planning to use air bags, it might mean that other auto makers will follow. We should contact air bag suppliers and look for collaborative opportunities.

Chapter 2

AIR BAG SYSTEMS INDUSTRY FORCES ANALYSIS FOR 1992

1992 Pie and Trend Chart Analysis

For 1992, we examined a total of eighty-seven articles and identified 528 concepts. Looking at the pie chart, we see that the governmental force continued to dominate the air bag systems industry (figure 2.7). In fact, the governmental force greatly outdistanced the technology force which was the second-place industry force. And the trend chart in figure 2.8 confirms the dominance of the governmental force. It dominated almost every month of 1992.

The governmental force topped all other forces during 1992 for a number of reasons. There were many complaints from motorists concerning air bag injuries, and the government was paying a lot of attention to these complaints. Also, the government was doing a lot more, generally, to learn about air bags and their limitations.

In the 1992 charts, both regulatory and management forces were larger than the marketing force. The increased management force probably reflects the attention organizations were giving to the government's plan to mandate front-seat air bags. Managers were probably taking actions to promote air bags and talking more about the air bag systems industry. Management activity shows up more prominently this year than last year in the charts.

Interestingly enough, technology tied with government for dominance during the last month of 1992 as shown in the trend chart (figure 2.8). We need to investigate new technology to determine what organizations in the industry are trying to develop technologically advanced air bag fabric.

Environmental Forces Analysis

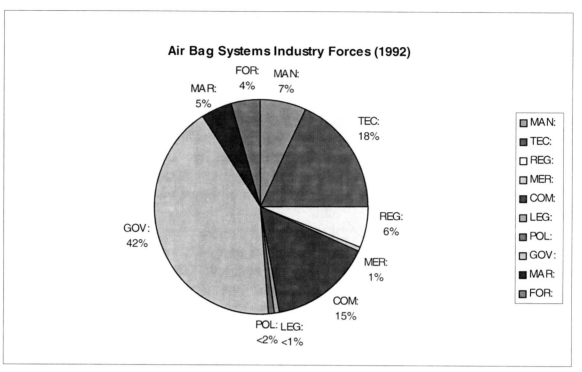

Fig. 2.7

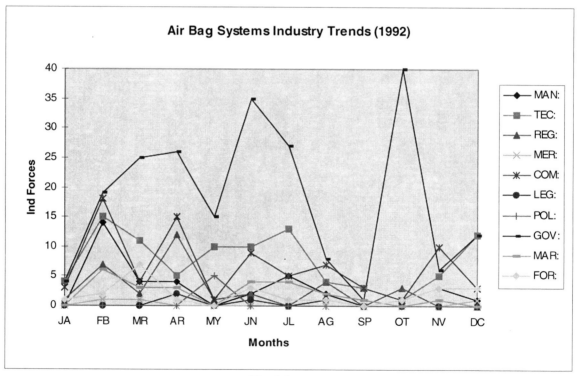

Fig. 2.8

Note: The above distribution and trend charts are associated with the 1992 environmental forces.

Chapter 2

1992 Extracted Concept Analysis

Below is a 1992 December concept that was taken from the concepts used to create the pie and trend charts in figures 2.7 and 2.8. The dominant force concept is shown for the most-frequently-mentioned keyword. The dominant force for 1992 was government. The most-frequently-mentioned government keyword was "admin." Therefore, the concept below was identified by the keyword "admin."

Only one concept is shown for December 1992 because all the concepts in December for the keyword "admin" and its derivatives addressed the air bag mandate. So, we didn't feel it necessary to discuss the other "admin" concepts for that month.

Dominant Environmental Force Concept

1992 Concept

Source: The Commercial Appeal (Memphis)
Date: December 15, 1992
Headline: U.S. Will Mandate Car Airbags by 1998

Concept Sentence: "The National Highway Traffic Safety Administration proposed the change to its automatic occupant protection standard."

Strategic Comment: There has been a competition between automatic seat belts and air bags since the passive restraint rule went into effect. However, it appears that the government believes that air bags are essential for safety. This presents an opportunity for our organization. We should look for collaborative opportunities with air bag suppliers.

AIR BAG SYSTEMS INDUSTRY FORCES ANALYSIS FOR 1993

1993 Pie and Trend Chart Analysis

For 1993, we examined a total of 187 articles and identified 840 concepts. We can see from the pie chart for 1993 that the technology force was the dominant force (figure 2.9), with the governmental force second. This represented a shift in dominance from 1992 when the governmental force was dominant. Actually, the shift in dominance was "anticipated" by the 1992 trend chart.

The 1993 trend chart (figure 2.10) also shows a shift in dominant force from 1992. Again, the shift is from government to technology. We should determine why the shift took place. (We assume that when a shift happens, it will continue into the future for at least one year.) If the shift is an indication of new technology, it is in our organization's best interest to determine what the technology is and how it can help or hurt us. Reviewing individual concepts will help us make that determination.

The marketing force was at its highest level (9 percent) since the beginning of our ten-year analysis period. This was probably because, by 1993, air bags were viewed as a good safety requirement. Thus, there was an increase in marketing activity by air bag systems organizations.

There were different types of research projects taking place in 1993 in the air bag systems area. As shown in the trend chart (figure 2.10), technology was either the leading force or pretty much tied for the leading force position in most months of the year. Since technology has taken over as the leading force, it would behoove our organization to determine what the new technology areas might be. We don't want to be at a disadvantage. We should review industry competitors' marketing material.

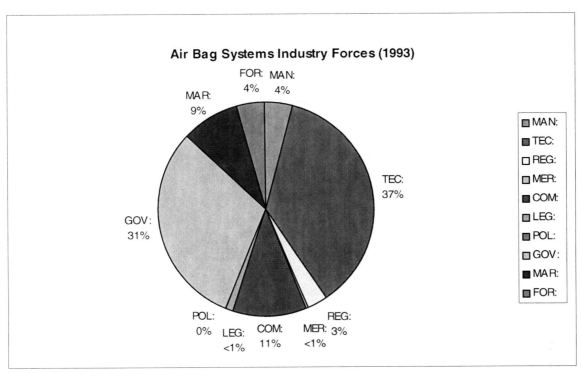

Fig. 2.9

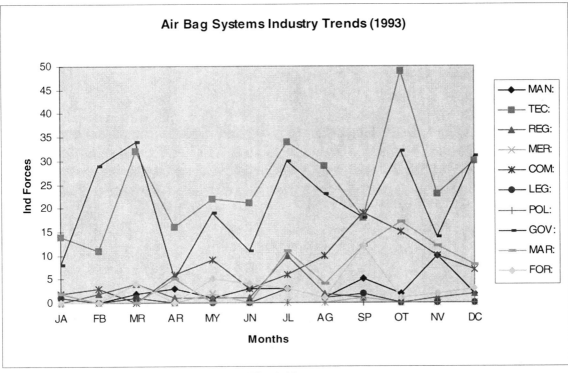

Fig. 2.10

Note: The above distribution and trend charts are associated with the 1993 environmental forces.

Environmental Forces Analysis

1993 Extracted Concept Analysis

The 1993 concepts support the technology force, since the technology force was the dominant force during 1993. December dominant force concepts are shown for the most-frequently-mentioned keyword. The most-frequently-mentioned technology keyword was "design." Therefore, the concepts below were identified by the keyword "design" and its derivatives. These concepts address research that was being done in the air bag systems industry. The concepts address add-on air bags, and how it might be possible to increase air bag safety with better design.

Dominant Environmental Force Concepts

1993 Concept 1

Source: Chicago Tribune
Date: December 26, 1993
Headline: Extra Cushion: Add-ons Offer Protection in Cars
without Factory Air Bags

Concept Sentence: "'Simply adding a bag and an inflator does not constitute the same level of protection we see as air bags that are designed as standard equipment,' said Chrysler spokesman Chris Preuss."

Strategic Comment: This concept indicates that there is some hesitancy concerning the use of add-on air bags. We should act with caution. There is already some controversy surrounding air bag injuries. So, we want to make sure that we don't put our organization in danger by associating it with air bags that might be more dangerous than factory-installed air bags.

1993 Concept 2

Source: Sacramento Bee
Date: December 20, 1993
Headline: No Air Bag in Hurley Vehicle

Concept Sentence: "In tandem, belts and air bags are designed to keep a driver's body as motionless as possible -- the primary lifesaving factor in sudden-impact crashes."

Strategic Comment: That it is known that air bags and seat belts work together to save lives is a boost to our organization. We believe that the air bag industry will be healthy for the foreseeable future, continuing to create opportunity for our organization.

1993 Concept 3

Source: The Washington Times
Date: December 17, 1993
Headline: Air Bags Differ in Construction, Mode of Activation but Consistently Save Lives

Concept Sentence: "The different fold designs modulate the way the bag inflates, though as yet there's no consensus on which type of fold is best."

Strategic Comment: We should work to improve our fabric technology so that we can be at the forefront in reducing air bag problems associated with the air bag fabric. One of the known problems is something called a "slap" problem. During air bag inflation, the motorist can be slapped, and the fold design can affect the nature of the slap. We should determine what our direct competitors are doing to reduce the slap problem. This could be an opportunity for our organization.

1993 Concept 4

Source: The Record
Date: December 10, 1993
Headline: N.J. Company Offers Retrofitted Air Bags

Concept Sentence: "Applied Safety said the system is designed to fit more than 40 models of cars and light trucks made from 1987 through 1994 by General Motors Corp., the Ford Motor Co., and Chrysler Corp."

Strategic Comment: We should contact organizations that are making retrofit air bags. We should look for possible collaborative opportunities. At the same time, we should be careful not to align ourselves with any retrofit air bag maker, since these air bags may not be as safe as factory installed air bags.

Environmental Forces Analysis

1993 Concept 5

Source: The New York Times
Date: December 8, 1993
Headline: Science Watch: Side Effect of Life-Saving Air Bags

Concept Sentence: "Still, other ophthalmologists who have treated air-bag accident victims say that improvements in the design of the devices might reduce the harm they can inflict to the eyes and face without diminishing their lifesaving attributes."

Strategic Comment: We want to do what we can to improve the air bag fabric technology so that we can reduce air bag injuries where possible. Improving air bag fabric technology can give us a competitive advantage and thus create opportunities for our organization.

1993 Concept 6

Source: Chicago Sun-Times
Date: December 1, 1993
Headline: Why Airbags, Kid Seats May Not Mix

Concept Sentence: "Picture a baby secured in a car seat designed to face rearward, properly restrained, in the front passenger seat of a car." (We reviewed parts of the article to learn more about this concept.)

Strategic Comment: Air bags in the front seat can endanger small children who are placed in child seats in those front seats. Our organization should do what it can to eliminate this danger to children. If we can find ways to eliminate these dangers, we can create opportunities for our organization.

Chapter 2

AIR BAG SYSTEMS INDUSTRY FORCES ANALYSIS FOR 1994

1994 Pie and Trend Chart Analysis

Figures 2.11 and 2.12 show the air bag systems industry forces for 1994. We examined 239 articles, identifying 1,304 concepts for 1994. Looking at the pie chart (figure 2.11), we see that the technology force is, again, the dominant force. Technology was the dominant force for most of the months in 1994 (figure 2.12). So the shift in dominant forces, first seen in 1993, continued to 1994. And the gap between the technology force and the governmental force increased in 1994 compared to 1993.

The marketing force was at its highest level, so far, relative to the other forces. As mentioned for 1993, organizations seemed to be spending more time marketing air bags during 1994. Our organization can try to determine what air bag systems makers are doing by reviewing their marketing material. We need to ferret out direct rivals and organizations that might offer collaborative opportunities.

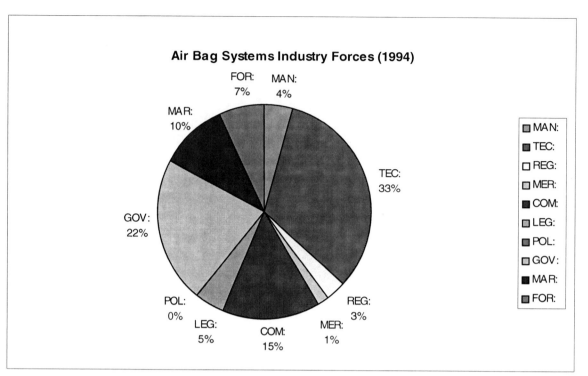

Fig. 2.11

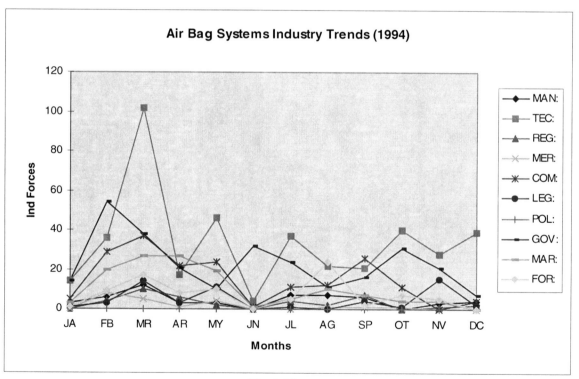

Fig. 2.12

Note: The above distribution and trend charts are associated with the 1994 environmental forces.

Chapter 2

1994 Extracted Concept Analysis

Below are December concepts from the 1994 articles that support the pie and trend charts. The dominant force was technology. Dominant force concepts are shown for the most-frequently-mentioned keyword. The most-frequently-mentioned technology keyword was "technology." Therefore, the concepts below were identified by the keyword "technology."

Most of the concepts for December 1994 deal with the study that showed motorists to be driving less safely now because of the use of air bags. This may represent an opportunity for our organization. We may be able to increase our name recognition by advocating safer driving.

Dominant Environmental Force Concepts

(The concepts below have duplicate information. Indeed two of the concepts are identical. The motorists' reliance on air bags became the dominant theme during December of 1994, and we wanted to emphasize that.)

1994 Concept 1

Source: The Phoenix Gazette
Date: December 27, 1994
Headline: Air-Bag Owners in More Crashes:
Study: Emboldened Drivers Think Technology Will Bail Them Out

Concept Sentence: "'They think technology [seat belt related technology] will bail them out.'"

Strategic Comment: See the comment at the end of the 1994 concepts. Since the concepts shown below for 1994 cover the same issue, only one strategic comment is given.

1994 Concept 2

Source: The Virginian-Pilot
Date: December 27, 1994
Headline: Drivers with Air Bags Take More Risks,
Crash More, Study Suggests

Concept Sentence: "'They think technology will bail them out.'"

Strategic Comment: See the comment at the bottom of the 1994 concepts.

1994 Concept 3

Source: Chicago Tribune
Date: December 27, 1994
Headline: Drivers with Air Bags Take Risks, Study Says

Concept Sentence: "'What it [the study] suggests is that air-bag drivers are driving in such a manner as to offset the effectiveness of the air bag,' Hoffer said." (George Hoffer is a Virginia Commonwealth University economist who was part of a group that researched crashes.)

Strategic Comment: This concept, and the others for December 1994, address one of the hazards of air bag usage: People take more chances with air bags. This concept was picked up by a number of papers. Indeed this concept was one of the most covered concepts during December of 1994. This is why we repeated the concept. This concept might represent an opportunity for our organization if we can figure out how our organization can take a lead in advising motorists to drive more safely. We may be able to get a reputation as a good corporate citizen.

Chapter 2

AIR BAG SYSTEMS INDUSTRY FORCES ANALYSIS FOR 1995

1995 Pie and Trend Chart Analysis

We examined 379 articles identifying 2,030 concepts for this year. We see in the pie chart that government is again the dominant force (figure 2.13). Looking at the trend chart (figure 2.14), it appears that the governmental force became dominant during the latter part of the year.

So, during the year, a shift in dominance actually occurred from technology to government. We should investigate the shift for opportunities and threats.

Note that the percentage of the pie share (figure 2.13) related to marketing forces declined. But there was an increase in the pie share for the litigation forces. It appears that air bags have been in use long enough for motorists to see the bad as well as the good associated with air bags.

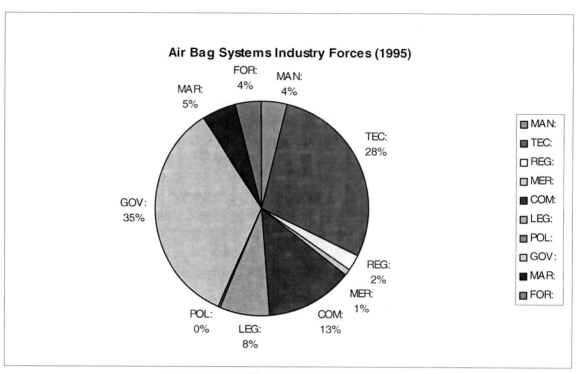

Fig. 2.13

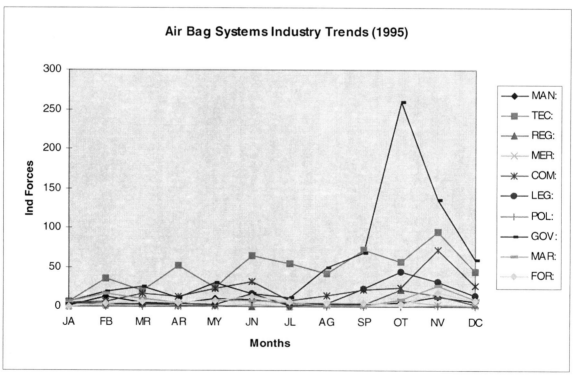

Fig. 2.14

Note: The above distribution and trend charts are associated with the 1995 environmental forces.

Chapter 2

1995 Extracted Concept Analysis

Although the government force took a bigger slice of the pie for 1995, technology was dominant for most of the year (see figure 2.14). Since technology was also dominant for most of 1994, we decided to treat technology as the dominant force for 1995. Therefore, concepts for technology are analyzed for 1995.

December dominant force concepts are shown for the most-frequently-mentioned keyword. The most-frequently-mentioned technology keyword was "design." Therefore, the concepts below were identified by the keyword "design" and its derivatives.

These concepts address an air bag related lawsuit, a car seat to protect motorists in rear-end collisions, and the side air bag, among other items.

Dominant Environmental Force Concepts

1995 Concept 1

Source: Chicago Tribune
Date: December 31, 1995
Headline: Keeping an Eye on Air-Bag Risks

Concept Sentence: "Vents in the bag allow the air to start escaping as soon as your head hits the bag to provide the cushioning effect."

Strategic Comment: Our organization needs to make sure that our fabric allows air bag systems to work properly. This includes air bag venting and other capabilities. Our organization is threatened if our fabric does not carry out its functions properly.

1995 Concept 2

Source: Pittsburgh Post-Gazette
Date: December 30, 1995
Headline: GM to Stand Trial for Lack of Air Bags in Older Cars

Concept Sentence: "Wilson's estate sued GM in Indiana state court, alleging the company was negligent for designing and selling a car that was not crashworthy since it did not contain an air bag."

Strategic Comment: This concept shows the importance the air bag has taken on in our country. This concept also highlights the opportunities in the air bag industry.

1995 Concept 3

Source: Roanoke Times & World News
Date: December 23, 1995
Headline: Arsenal Filling Air Bags: Propellant Powers
Commercial Project

Concept Sentence: "Precision Fabrics Group Inc.'s Vinton plant, which makes industrial fabrics, said in June it will manufacture the fabric for a newly designed air bag." (We went back to the original article to manually retrieve some concept text.)

Strategic Comment: This concept highlights one of our direct rivals. We need to investigate the organization and determine if it makes a superior fabric. This organization most likely represents a threat to our organization.

1995 Concept 4

Source: The Fresno Bee
Date: December 16, 1995
Headline: Rear Impact Protection from a 'Mitt': Front and
Side Air Bags Lead to the Idea of a Catcher's Mitt
for Back Seats

Concept Sentence: "General Motors Delphi Automotive Systems (basically GM's parts and components operation) has come up with a car seat designed to aid occupants in rear-enders."

Strategic Comment: We need to look into this concept. It might represent an opportunity if we can collaborate with organizations making this seat.

1995 Concept 5

Source: The Atlanta Journal and Constitution
Date: December 8, 1995

Headline: The Drive Toward Safety:
Auto Show Highlights: Check out the Latest in Technology - from an
Emergency Rescue Device That Uses Satellites to a Concept Car
That Can Deploy 17 Air Bags in a Crash

Concept Sentence: "A concept car making the rounds of some auto shows can deploy 17 air bags from the car's front, sides and top." (We went back to the original article to manually retrieve some concept text.)

Strategic Comment: We should look for opportunities to collaborate with side and top (of the car) air bag systems suppliers as well as front air bag system suppliers. This concept presents more opportunities for our organization.

1995 Concept 6

Source: The Salt Lake Tribune
Date: December 02, 1995
Headline: Air-bag Maker Campaigns for Safety
Air-Bag Maker to Teach Safety Program

Concept Sentence: "Do not . . . retrofit older cars with air bags, . . . protection depends on the bag being specifically designed for a specific vehicle."

Strategic Comment: We should be careful not to form any alliance with a retrofit air bag maker. If the retrofit air bags prove to be unsafe, and we are associated with them, this association could negatively affect our organization. This would be a threat.

1995 Concept 7

Source: Star Tribune (Minneapolis)
Date: December 2, 1995
Headline: FYI: Side Air Bags Are Next in Passive Restraints

Concept Sentence: "Seat belts prevent occupants from being thrown sideways across the car but provide no protection for the head and shoulder of a driver or passenger on the side that is struck by another vehicle." (We went back to the original article to manually retrieve some concept text.)

Strategic Comment: We need to determine what organizations are planning to supply side air bags. The use of side air bags in automobiles presents an opportunity for our organization.

1995 Concept 8

Source: Seattle Post-Intelligencer
Date: December 1, 1995
Headline: Ford Will Be First of Big Three to Offer Side-
                Impact Air Bags

Concept Sentence: "Ford is the first of Detroit's Big Three automakers to publicly commit to the additional safety devices designed to protect against deadly head and chest injuries."

Strategic Comment: That Ford is committing to side air bags is a sign that air bags have a bright future. The air bag systems industry will continue to present opportunities for our organization. We should contact Ford and its air bag suppliers to find collaborative opportunities.

Chapter 2

AIR BAG SYSTEMS INDUSTRY FORCES ANALYSIS FOR 1996

1996 Pie and Trend Chart Analysis

The pie chart shows that government was the dominant force for 1996 (figure 2.15). We examined 1,050 articles, identifying 7,289 concepts for 1996. We can see that the dominant force trend (figure 2.16) changed from a virtual tie between the governmental and technology forces to a lead by the governmental force. In fact, there is a gap of over 30 percentage points between the governmental and technology forces (figure 2.15). And the trend chart shows that most of this gap was achieved during the last six months of 1996.

Although the government was still pushing for air bags, there was a lot of turmoil in the industry. The governmental force was the highest it had ever been. This was probably because air bags caused a number of injuries, and these injuries were encouraging governmental activity. The government was looking into the injuries and investigating the usefulness of air bag cut-off switches.

The regulatory force was three times as large as the marketing force in 1996. For most previous years, the marketing force was larger than the regulatory force. The regulatory force was relatively large for 1996, probably because the government was establishing guidelines for cut-off switches. These guidelines gave rise to other government related activity. We should monitor the governmental activity, read reports when we can acquire them, and emphasize safety features as we design our air bag fabric.

Environmental Forces Analysis

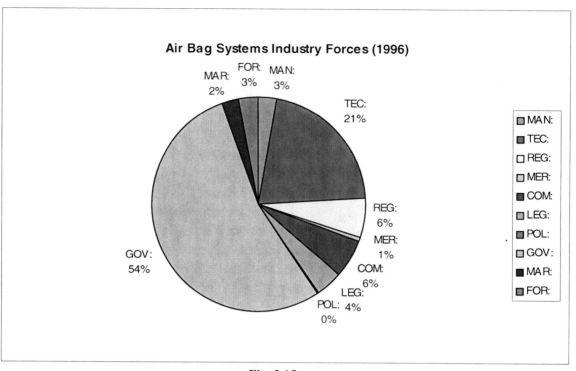

Fig. 2.15

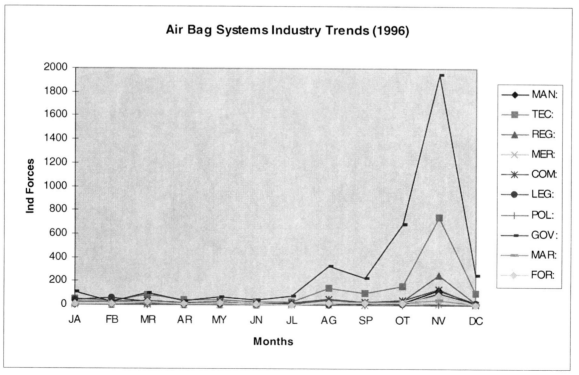

Fig. 2.16

Note: The above distribution and trend charts are associated with the 1996 environmental forces.

64

Chapter 2

1996 Extracted Concept Analysis

For 1996, the dominant force was the government. Among the following concepts, you will note that there was talk about air bag dangers and how air bags may have been over-sold. It was also felt by some that auto manufactures didn't use the best air bag design. Also, there was talk about allowing motorists to disconnect air bags.

Dominant December force concepts are shown for the most-frequently-mentioned keyword. The most-frequently-mentioned government keyword was "government." Therefore, the concepts below were identified by the keyword "government."

Dominant Environmental Force Concepts

1996 Concept 1

Source: Chicago Tribune
Date: December 5, 1996
Headline: Air Bag Dangers

Concept Sentence: "But the federal government's obstinate defense of a 'safety' device that can kill or seriously injure is turning Orwellian."

Strategic Comment: This concept indicates a threat to our organization. Air bags have caused injuries and actually killed some people. If these problems cause any relaxation in the government mandate, the relaxation will threaten our organization's future. We need to monitor these activities.

1996 Concept 2

Source: Denver Rocky Mountain News
Date: December 5, 1996
Headline: Hot Air Inflated Air Bag Safety

Concept Sentence: "Because the government decided I [someone upset over air bag requirements] had to have an air bag, I cannot put any of my three children in the front seat."

Strategic Comment: There are some feelings that the air bag is over-hyped. And some people think that they have lost some freedom because of the air bag rules. These feelings represent threats to our organization.

1996 Concept 3

Source: The Detroit News
Date: December 05, 1996
Headline: Deflating the Hot Air about Air Bags

Concept Sentence: "The Naderites and other 'public interest' types pressured the government to force automakers to install 'passive restraints.'" (This was a mistake in the opinion of some.)

Strategic Comment: This concept represents more negative reaction to air bags. Some think that the government is trying to save motorists from themselves, even if the motorists don't want to be saved. This attitude threatens our organization. However, as long as the government mandate stays in place, there will be users of air bags and buyers of air bag fabric.

1996 Concept 4

Source: The Detroit News
Date: December 05, 1996
Headline: Investigators Don't Rule Out Air Bag's Role in
                Oakland Death

Concept Sentence: "Air-bag risks to youngsters and small passengers have been the subject of a recent review by vehicle manufacturers and the federal government."

Strategic Comment: This concept points out the risks associated with air bags. These risks and the discussion of air bag risks represent a threat to our organization. We should continue to monitor governmental activities.

Chapter 2

1996 Concept 5

Source: Idaho Falls Post Register
Date: December 05, 1996
Headline: Detroit, Not Fed, Ruined Air Bags

Concept Sentence: "'From my perspective, the government regulations worked just fine and the automobile manufacturers did not carry out their duty of care.'" (This is according to Joan Claybrook, former Administrator of the National Highway Traffic Safety Administration, who pushed for air bags.)

Strategic Comment: This concept shows some of the words of a defender of the air bag regulations. Claybrook is influential. As long as influential individuals defend the air bag system, threats to the air bag systems industry and our organization will be eased.

1996 Concept 6

Source: The Phoenix Gazette
Date: December 5, 1996
Headline: The Risk and Necessity of Air Bags: Disconnect
                Option Puts Passenger in Greater Danger

Concept Sentence: "After weeks of intense media coverage of the risks of serious injury from inflating air bags, the federal government is proposing to allow repair shops to disconnect bags if car owners want this done."

Strategic Comment: This is a threat to our organization. If the government allows motorists to disconnect air bags, this could be a sign that the government may loosen its mandated passive restraint rule. We should monitor this activity and take part in activities that show air bag usage in a positive light.

1996 Concept 7

Source: The Plain Dealer
Date: December 5, 1996
Headline: Be Smarter than Your Airbag

Concept Sentence: "Disconnecting these airbags to protect small adults and children who might be injured by their impact, as some consumer advocates now recommend, is dumber." (We went back to the original article to manually retrieve some concept text.)

Strategic Comment: This concept shows that some people think it is dumb to disconnect air bags. Where possible, we need to support groups pushing air bags.

1996 Concept 8

Source: The Post and Courier (Charleston, SC)
Date: December 4, 1996
Headline: Still Time for Public to Have Say on Air-Bags

Concept Sentence: "But air bags have long been a federal government fetish, forced on a reluctant auto industry and oversold to the public."

Strategic Comment: This concept indicates that some believe the government oversold air bags. This kind of thinking represents a threat to our organization if it causes the government to back off on the air bag mandate.

1996 Concept 9

Source: The Dallas Morning News
Date: December 3, 1996
Headline: Safety First or Safety Worst? Air Bags in Autos
Have Saved Lives, but Also Have Caused Fatalities

Concept Sentence: "Earlier this year, the parents group began lobbying the government and manufacturers for prominent warning labels."

Strategic Comment: This concept represents a threat to our organization. This parents organization is lobbying for warning labels on air bags. If the air bag continues to get bad press, the government could relax its air bag mandate. We need to learn more about this group. And we need to do what we can to make our fabric as safe as possible. We also need to help publicize the benefits of air bags.

1996 Concept 10

Source:	The Washington Times
Date:	December 3, 1996
Headline:	Poor Journalism Does Not Add to the Air-Bag Debate

Concept Sentence: "As a government official 17 years ago, I [Joan Claybrook] supplied them with data that recommended a number of design options, including dual-inflation air bags."

Strategic Comment: This concept addresses the feelings of a former government official about the air bag choices the manufacturers made. This official indicated that the manufacturers made a poor design choice. That there may be better ways to design air bags may create opportunities for our organization, if these better designs are pursued by air bag systems makers. We just need to make sure our organization plays a role in any re-design efforts.

1996 Concept 11

Source:	Asheville Citizen-Times
Date:	December 2, 1996
Headline:	Airbag Problem Requires Quick Fix

Concept Sentence: "Meanwhile, USA Today reported that the National Highway Traffic Safety Administration will rewrite regulations to allow motorists to have their air bags disconnected by dealers and mechanics." (We went back to the original article to manually retrieve some text.)

Strategic Comment: This concept represents a threat to our organization. If motorists don't have to use air bags, it could negatively affect our organization.

1996 Concept 12

Source:	The Times-Picayune
Date:	December 2, 1996
Headline:	Air Bag Hazard

Concept Sentence: "But if they [air bags] are to bear the imprimatur of government safety officials, steps must be taken to ensure that the public is protected against a device that is intended to protect them."

Strategic Comment: This concept makes it clear that air bags must get safer if the government is going to continue to endorse them. Although this concept is somewhat negative, it still highlights an opportunity for our organization. Air bags will be around for a long time since the government will probably continue to endorse air bags.

1996 Concept 13

Source:	The Washington Times
Date:	December 2, 1996
Headline:	Painful Battle over Car Air Bags Certain to Inflate Local Economy

Concept Sentence: "Automakers also want changes so they won't be held liable when their own safety devices backfire."

Strategic Comment: This concept presents a threat to our organization. Organizations are asking for ways to avoid being held liable when the air bags don't work as desired. This means that automakers are worried about the air bag. This might cause the automakers to stop pushing air bags, which would be a threat to our organization. We should monitor this activity.

1996 Concept 14

Source:	Seattle Post-Intelligencer
Date:	December 1, 1996
Headline:	Joint Solution on Air Bags

Concept Sentence: "Research of government documents conducted by Hearst Newspapers last month disclosed that industry and government officials have known for more than 20 years that air bags posed dangers to children and small adults."

Strategic Comment: This concept indicates that the industry knew about the air bag problems 20 years ago. This could be a threat to our organization if there is a public backlash against air bags.

1996 Concept 15

Source: The Boston Globe
Date: December 1, 1996
Headline: Air-Bag Fears Could Threaten Common Sense

Concept Sentence: "Senate Commerce Committee members say they will now investigate whether the government is moving fast enough to save children from air bags."

Strategic Comment: This concept indicates that the Senate is looking into the air bag problems. Although we all want air bags to be safe for children, this concept is a threat to our organization. Because this kind of activity will bring unwanted attention to our industry, we need to monitor the activity and do what we can to make air bags safer.

1996 Concept 16

Source: Los Angeles Times
Date: December 1, 1996
Headline: Air Bags

Concept Sentence: "Do air bags indeed save more people who are also belted with lap and shoulder harnesses?" (We went back to the original article to manually retrieve some concept text.)

Strategic Comment: This concept questions the added benefit of air bags. This kind of speculation can be a threat to our organization. We need to make sure we get reports which show the benefits and dangers of air bags. We need to make the benefits known to air bag system users and potential users. We need to help minimize the dangers.

1996 Concept 17

Source: The Plain Dealer
Date: December 1, 1996
Headline: Air Bag's Creator Still Keeping the Faith

Concept Sentence: "But the problems started when the government tried to jam them down people's throats." (This is according to William Carey, sometimes called the father of the air bag.)

Strategic Comment: William Carey says that the air bag problems could have been avoided if there had been better cooperation between auto organizations and the government. That there was a lack of cooperation can create an opportunity in the industry for us now. We should work within the industry to strengthen cooperation. This may increase our name recognition.

Chapter 2

AIR BAG SYSTEMS INDUSTRY FORCES ANALYSIS FOR 1997

1997 Pie and Trend Chart Analysis

The dominant force continues to be the government (figures 2.17 and 2.18). We examined 1,308 articles for 1997, identifying 8,392 concepts. The gap between the governmental force and the second-place technology force increased in 1997 from 1996. This increase indicates that even more attention was being paid to the air bag systems industry by the government than before.

Looking at the trend chart (figure 2.18), it appears that the governmental force dominated all months during 1997. This government dominance is likely to continue into 1998. We should note that the governmental force displayed its most dominance during the last quarters of 1995, 1996, and 1997.

There continued to be a lot of regulatory force activity in 1997, relative to many of the other environmental forces. The regulatory force was the fourth largest force (figure 2.17). There was still talk about injuries and the possibility of giving motorists the right to deactivate air bags. This talk, no doubt, produced some of the regulatory activity.

We should get air bag systems reports from the government. We should design our air bag materials with safety in mind.

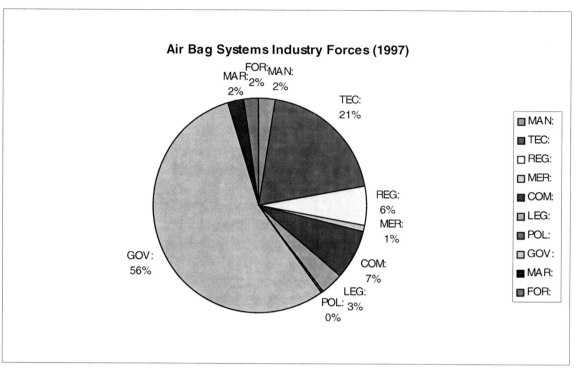

Fig. 2.17

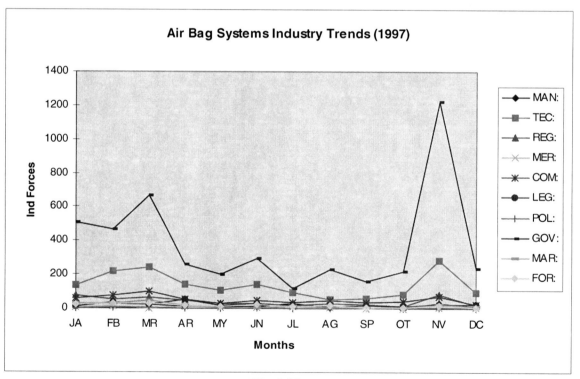

Fig. 2.18

Note: The above distribution and trend charts are associated with the 1997 environmental forces.

Chapter 2

1997 Extracted Concept Analysis

The government has allowed some people to deactivate their air bags. The government was also establishing rules for lower power air bag inflation that could reduce air bag related injuries.

Dominant force concepts are shown for the most-frequently-mentioned keyword. The most-frequently-mentioned government keyword was "government." Therefore, the concepts below were identified by the keyword "government" and its derivatives.

The concepts addressed for December '97 include the dangers of air bags to children, the process of getting air bags deactivated, and the fact that fewer motorists than expected requested that their air bags be deactivated.

Dominant Environmental Force Concepts

1997 Concept 1

Source: Chicago Tribune
Date: December 29, 1997
Headline: Protecting Us to Death: U.S. Air-Bag Policy Puts
Children at Risk

Concept Sentence: "And we have a government that not only mandates this device's use [the air bag's] but denies us the right and the opportunity to offer our loved ones protection from its deadly force."

Strategic Comment: This concept indicates that some people are still upset over the government's air bag mandate. This represents a threat to our organization.

1997 Concept 2

Source: The Boston Globe
Date: December 27, 1997
Headline: Auto Makers Responsible for Flaws of Air Bags:
Letters to the Editor

Concept Sentence: "The hazards of air bags come from deliberate design choices made by the companies, not the lack of government testing."

Strategic Comment: This concept presents an opportunity for our organization. If we can help make the air bag safer, we can help our bottom line.

1997 Concept 3

Source:	Charleston Daily Mail
Date:	December 27, 1997
Headline:	Air Bags - Safety Gets Lost in the Worry over Being Sued If You Do, Sued If You Don't

Concept Sentence: "Parents and short people who want to remove these dangers [associated with the use of air bags] from their cars must get the permission of government to undo the do-gooders' handiwork."

Strategic Comment: This concept presents a threat to our organization. We should do what we can to make the air bag fabric safer.

1997 Concept 4

Source:	Press Journal (Vero Beach, CA)
Date:	December 27, 1997
Headline:	Fewer Air-Bag on-off Requests than Expected

Concept Sentence: "WASHINGTON - Far fewer motorists are requesting government permission to install on-off switches for their air bags than safety officials had feared."

Strategic Comment: This concept embodies good news for our organization. Many people probably believe that the advantages of air bags outweigh the disadvantages. Also, once air bags are installed in automobiles, most motorists probably don't feel that it's necessary to have air bags deactivated.

Chapter 2

1997 Concept 5

Source: The Detroit News
Date: December 26, 1997
Headline: Design May Guide Airbag Safety: Companies Credit
Low Force of Deployment, Consumer Education
for Their Clean Records

Concept Sentence: "Also, why hasn't the federal government recorded a single airbag death or serious injury to an adult or child in a BMW, Honda, Acura or Audi?"

Strategic Comment: We need to look at the air bag systems used by the above automakers. We need to see if these organizations' air bags are safer. We also should look for collaborative opportunities with these automakers' air bag systems' suppliers.

1997 Concept 6

Source: Star Tribune (Minneapolis, MN)
Date: December 21, 1997
Headline: How Short Should You Be before Turning off Air
Bag?

Concept Sentence: "When considering short people, the panel conducted an exhaustive search on government data and medical research, Jolly said." (Dr. Tilman Jolly is chairman of the National Conference on Medical Indications for Air Bag Disconnection.)

Strategic Comment: We need to look into this research. We need to determine if there is any way for us to improve air bag safety, especially with regard to short people, by modifying our air bag fabric.

1997 Concept 7

Source: The Buffalo News
Date: December 19, 1997
Headline: U.S. Asks Detailed Data on Air Bag Performance
Safety: Panel Tells Makers Information Is Needed
to Shape New Regulations

Concept Sentence: "A government safety agency is demanding comprehensive information from the nation's leading auto manufacturers about the design and performance of their air bags."

Strategic Comment: We need to monitor the activity described in this concept. We should try to review the information. We want to determine what part, if any, the air bag fabric plays in the overall safety of air bags.

1997 Concept 8

Source: The Charleston Gazette
Date: December 19, 1997
Headline: Air Bag Deactivation Forms Now Available

Concept Sentence: "To get the government's permission to install the switch, motorists must pledge that they . . . [cannot] avoid placing rear-facing infant seats in the front passenger seat." (There are other reasons one could give to try to get permission. This is a legitimate reason related to child safety. We went back to the original article to manually retrieve some concept text.)

Strategic Comment: Any time the government relaxes its air bag usage requirement, it is a threat to our organization. We need to work with those organizations that are trying to overcome the child-related air bag problems.

1997 Concept 9

Source: The Detroit News
Date: December 18, 1997
Headline: More Infants Buckled in Front:
Study: Drivers Still Put Young Kids in Path of Passenger Air Bags,
Despite Warnings

Concept Sentence: "Release of the study coincided with the government's effort to begin processing motorists' requests for air bag on-off switches."

Strategic Comment: This concept indicates that motorists are still putting children in the front seats, subjecting them to the dangers of air bags. It is a threat to our organization if children continue to be injured or killed by air bags. The injuries may cause the government to relax its air bag mandate.

1997 Concept 10

Source: The Buffalo News
Date: December 17, 1997
Headline: Requests to Deactivate Air Bags Reported As Less than 1,000

Concept Sentence: "The numbers suggest that an educational campaign by the government safety groups and the auto industry to persuade most people to keep the devices connected is working."

Strategic Comment: This concept indicates that with effort, the industry can prevent motorists from wanting to deactivate air bags. We should become involved in air bag educational activities. Better air bag education for motorists can reduce business threats to our organization.

1997 Concept 11

Source: The Tampa Tribune
Date: December 15, 1997
Headline: Making An Impact: Breed Technologies, Elbowing
                 into the Upper Ranks of Auto Safety System
                 Providers, Offers a Solution to a Deadly Air-Bag
                 Dilemma

Concept Sentence: "The federal government expects to issue a proposal on advanced air-bag systems in the first half of next year, though it doesn't expect full implementation until 2002." (We went back to the original article to manually retrieve some concept text.)

Strategic Comment: This concept presents an opportunity to our organization. We should contact Breed Technologies to determine if there are collaborative opportunities.

1997 Concept 12

Source: Chicago Tribune
Date: December 14, 1997
Headline: Hold the Hype on Air Bags, Please

Concept Sentence: "Neither hunting nor parachuting had the media, consumer activists and government regulators chomping at the bit to rid the country of shotguns or parachutes."

Strategic Comment: This concept drives home the fact that we should not throw out air bags as an important safety device. This is a good sentiment. It indicates that, in the minds of some, there are different ways of looking at air bag injury problems.

1997 Concept 13

Source: Chicago Tribune
Date: December 7, 1997
Headline: U.S. Doctors Urge Motorists to Stick with Air Bags

Concept Sentence: "Jolly [Tilman Jolly, associate professor of emergency medicine at the George Washington University Medical Center] and others defended the use of air bags after the government said consumers will be able to install on/off switches for the air bags in their vehicles in specific cases."

Strategic Comment: This concept presents good news for our organization. The fact that doctors are advising people to use air bags means that most people will probably continue to use air bags. The government probably won't relax its air bag mandate.

1997 Concept 14

Source: The Chattanooga Times
Date: December 3, 1997
Headline: The Nanny and the Air Bag

Concept Sentence: "But if a 5-foot, 110-pound woman can be killed or seriously injured by a deploying air bag, why does she have to ask the federal government for permission to deactivate the thing?"

Strategic Comment: This concept presents comments that are not good for our industry. We should monitor any action the government may take to relax its air bag mandate. If there is relaxation, this could represent a threat to our organization.

1997 Concept 15

Source: The Record (Bergen County, NJ)
Date: December 3, 1997
Headline: Dangerous Action on Airbags

Concept Sentence: "Instead of backing away, the government should mandate that automobile companies enact a standard that will ensure a higher survival rate of motorists in airbag-equipped vehicles."

Strategic Comment: If more people believe in this concept, we will continue to have opportunities in this industry.

AIR BAG SYSTEMS INDUSTRY FORCES ANALYSIS FOR 1998

1998 Pie and Trend Chart Analysis

We examined 795 articles for 1998, identifying 5,566 concepts. As seen in past years, the government continued to play the dominant role in the air bag systems industry. This is shown in the pie and trend charts (figures 2.19 and 2.20). Although the governmental force was generally larger than the other forces, there was a decline in the size of the governmental activities compared to 1997.

There was also a decrease in technology related activity. And it is worth noting that the percentage of the "pie" taken by the litigation force was at or near its highest level in 1998 when compared to previous years.

As we said above, the government was still the dominant force in 1997. In 1998, air bags are still mandated, and more and more air bags are being put into new automobiles. However, the government has received complaints about the deployment of air bags which could have been associated with the increase in litigation activity. We at **Mythical Air Bag Materials** should insure that there is nothing in the design of our air bag fabric that could prompt someone to sue our organization.

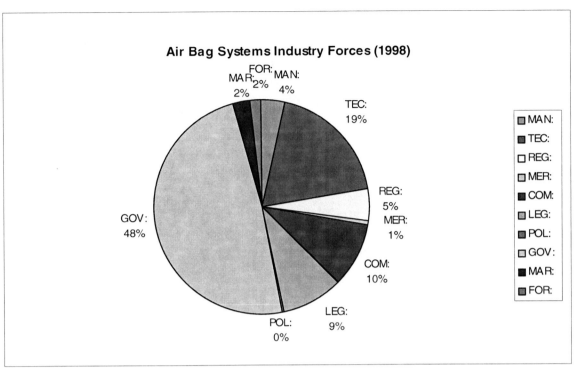

Fig. 2.19

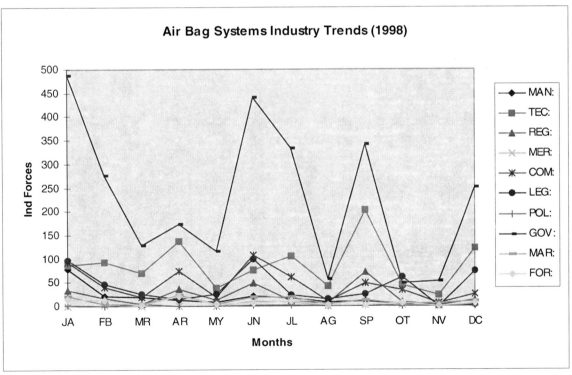

Fig. 2.20

Note: The above distribution and trend charts are associated with the 1998 environmental forces.

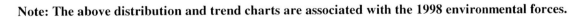

1998 Extracted Concept Analysis

There continued to be negative information about the use of air bags in automobiles as some of the December concepts below will indicate. Dominant force concepts are shown for the most-frequently-mentioned keyword. The dominant force was government. The most-frequently-mentioned government keyword was "government." Therefore, the concepts below were identified by the keyword "government" and its derivatives.

There was some concern that newer, depowered air bags would not protect motorists as well as the original air bags. But many of the '98 concepts point to a study showing that the depowered air bags offer as much protection as the original air bags.

Dominant Environmental Force Concepts

1998 Concept 1

Source: Press Journal (Vero Beach, CA)
Date: December 26, 1998
Headline: Study Shows Depowered Air Bags Work

Concept Sentence: "Data from depowered air-bag crashes, which the industry is helping to collect for the government, could play a role in National Highway Traffic Safety Administration decisions."

Strategic Comment: We need to get the results of these studies. We should adjust our fabric construction so that it meets any safety standards.

1998 Concept 2

Source: The Press-Enterprise (Riverside, Ca)
Date: December 26, 1998
Headline: A Softer Explosion: Second-Generation Air Bags in
                 Vehicles Are Supposed to Eliminate Accidental
                 Deaths Because They Don't Have the Force of the
                 First Bags

Concept Sentence: "But government and insurance safety experts and automakers say the lifesaving devices still can be dangerous -- even deadly -- if motorists don't take the proper precautions." (We went back to the original article to manually retrieve some concept text.)

Strategic Comment: There has been a reduction in the force of inflating air bags and they are now safer. This concept, however, indicates that some think that air bags may still be dangerous. This is a threat to our organization.

1998 Concept 3

Source: Chicago Tribune
Date: December 20, 1998
Headline: Depowered Air Bags Appear to Do the Job

Concept Sentence: "The National Highway Traffic Safety Administration has made public some information on 115 crashes involving depowered air bags installed in most new autos in the last year." (We went back to the original text to manually retrieve some concept text and learn more from the available information.)

Strategic Comment: This concept indicates that lower power air bags are working. This is good for our organization, since it will probably mean that people will continue to use air bags.

1998 Concept 4

Source: Press Journal (Vero Beach, FL)
Date: December 19, 1998
Headline: Experts See Mixed Verdicts in Air-Bag Death Suits

Concept Sentence: "Automakers determine for themselves the speed at which air bags should deploy, and the federal government repeatedly has declined to set a minimum."

Strategic Comment: This concept may present an opportunity for our organization. We need to determine what the optimum speed for deployment is. We need to determine if the optimum speed creates any fabric problems. We should collaborate with those organizations supplying air bags which deploy at the optimum speeds—especially if there is a way to use knowledge of the optimum speed to our fabric-design advantage.

1998 Concept 5

Source: Press Journal (Vero Beach, CA)
Date: December 14, 1998
Headline: Florida Tops List for Air Bag Deaths

Concept Sentence: "On the other hand, the government estimates nearly 3,500 Americans are alive today because of the more than 2.6 million air bags that have deployed."

Strategic Comment: This concept gives some good news. And it represents an opportunity and threat for our organization. We need to determine why Florida has the most air bag deaths. We need to determine if air bag fabric ever played any role in the deaths. If it turns out that fabric, somehow, is part of the problem, this would be bad news. But with more analysis of the problem, we may be able to improve our air bag fabric.

1998 Concept 6

Source: The Cincinnati Enquirer
Date: December 11, 1998
Headline: Less Forceful Air Bags Still Afford Protection

Concept Sentence: "Air bags redesigned to avoid killing shorter women in minor crashes appear to be forceful enough to protect larger adults in more severe accidents, government data indicate."

Strategic Comment: This concept presents good news for our organization. The newer air bags appear to be protecting large as well as small adults. This news may ease some of the negative press associated with air bags.

1998 Concept 7

Source: Press Journal (Vero Beach, CA)
Date: December 5, 1998
Headline: New Rules Sought for Airbags

Chapter 2

Concept Sentence: "WASHINGTON - The automobile industry still favors putting so-called smart airbags in its products but has asked the federal government to rewrite proposed rules on how the systems would be tested and expected to perform."

Strategic Comment: This concept presents good news for our industry. It indicates that both the government and automakers have faith in air bags. Thus, there is a good future for the industry.

Environmental Forces Analysis

Environmental Forces Historical Perspective

At this point, we have gained ten years' worth of knowledge concerning the air bag systems environment. (Figure 2.21 shows the dominant forces and the associated percentages for the 1989–1998 ten-year period. Each data point on the chart represents the end-of-the-year force.) We can use this knowledge in making strategic plans for the future.

For example, we see that the government is generally the dominant force in the air bag systems environment, while technology is typically in second place. Therefore, we should monitor government activities that are related to our industry. Generally, the government is working to push the use of air bags. Hence, governmental force dominance is a good thing for our organization.

Also, for the technology-dominant years, the marketing force appears to be somewhat inversely correlated with the technology force. We should focus on those strong competitors who appear to be cutting back on marketing. Analyzing these organizations may alert us to new technology and allow us to gain a competitive advantage. In some years (1996 for example), as the regulatory force increases, the marketing force decreases. We may be able to gain a competitive advantage by increasing our marketing activity whenever the government increases its regulatory activity. We may be able to increase this activity without being noticed by our competitors, since they may be more preoccupied with the regulatory activity than with us.

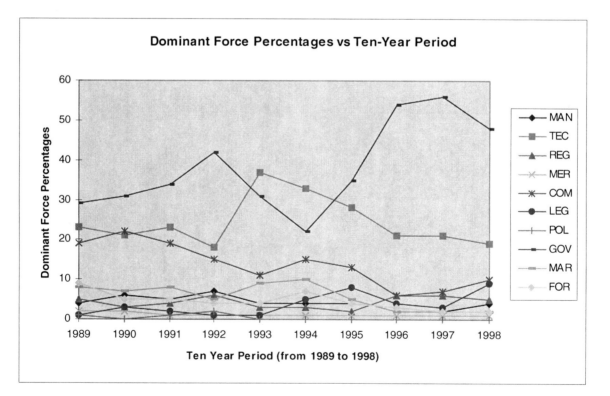

Fig. 2.21

Chapter 2

SUMMARY

Text mining software can be used to extract environmental forces concepts. We can use visualization methods to analyze these environmental forces concepts as a group and read the concepts individually to assess their strategic importance. Strategic analysts like to look ahead into the future, but it also makes sense to look back in time to determine what major forces have been at work in an industry. A ten-year period is a good period to look at when analyzing an industry. One of the benefits of text mining is that it can quickly deliver a large amount of industry historical environmental forces concepts for analysis.

The resulting concepts can provide useful insights for an organization. Analyzing the concepts in the form of distribution and trend charts can enable an organization to determine what the dominant environmental force is. Analyzing the individual concepts can enable an organization to determine specific strategic opportunities and threats.

By analyzing the environmental forces charts, we can determine if political forces are driving governmental forces, and we can determine if governmental forces are driving regulatory forces. An analysis of the environmental forces charts allows us to determine if the government, technology, or some other force is the major force within the organization's external environment. The environmental forces charts provide us with information on the interaction of forces within a year, and help us determine if one year's trends can predict environmental events for the next year.

For the air bag systems industry environment, the government was the dominant force for most of our ten-year period (1989–1998). The government was dominant for the first four years of the period. Technology became dominant during 1993 and remained dominant through 1994. In 1995, the governmental force again became dominant and remained so throughout the final three years of the ten-year period.

When performing an environmental force analysis, you can look at the force charts to determine the correlation between forces. Individual concept analysis supports the force chart analysis by allowing you to determine what activities really influence the charts. This analysis gives you some idea of what specific opportunities and threats exist within your business environment.

Chapter 3   Competitor Analysis Techniques

CHAPTER OVERVIEW

This chapter introduces you to some of the key aspects of this book's competitor analysis techniques. We first discuss typical business objectives and typical business strategies. We show questions that should be asked and answered to determine an organization's strategic capability. We talk about ways of identifying strategically capable competitors. And we list twenty strategically capable competitors and their related concepts that were generated with the help of text mining methods. The competitors are the air bag systems industry competitors used in the scenario and simulation analysis exercises shown in chapter 6.

COMPETITOR ANALYSIS

There are at least five elements you should assess, if possible, when analyzing a competitor's motives: The background of the Chief Executive Officer (CEO), and the organization's business objectives, assumptions, current business strategy, and business capabilities.

For example, if you know something about the background of your competitor's CEO, you may be in a position to accurately predict the types of moves your competitor might make. If you know your competitor's business objectives, you might have some insight into why your competitor is making a specific move. And if you know the assumptions, strategy and capabilities of your competitor, you are likely to understand how its executives and managers feel about their competitive position in the industry, and how well they can take advantage of business opportunities and navigate threats. In order to help us recognize or guess competitor motives, we decided to establish a set of common business objectives and a set of common business strategies. We show you these below.

Competitor Analysis Techniques

Business Objectives

It is important to note that most organizations—for-profit and not-for-profit—need to "make a profit" or have excess funds at the end of the year. Usually, organizations need to achieve this "excess funds" status in order to realize their missions. To achieve this status, organizations usually establish objectives.

For the discussions and exercises in this book, we assume that there are seven common basic objectives from which an organization is likely to choose its own business objectives. These objectives are introduced below and discussed further in chapter 4. We assume that a business organization will establish one or more of the following as its objectives:

- Achieve Low-Price Position

- Specialize in a Market or Market Segment

- Sell the Top Quality Product or Service

- Achieve Vertical Integration

- Become the Technological Leader

- Obtain Brand Name Identification

- Become a Value Added Provider (or Add Service to the Product Line)

As we said, we will use these seven objectives for the discussions and exercises in this book. However, for our day-to-day business intelligence analysis, we now often add two more objectives to our list of basic objectives. The two additional objectives are "expand market" and "obtain capital."

An organization may need to expand its market to improve its profits. To expand its market, the organization might decide to sell its existing products or services to new customers, or the organization might try to sell new products or services to its current customers. Or the organization might try to sell new products to new customers.

Similarly, an organization might need to obtain capital to grow its business. To do this, the organization could borrow money or decide to sell shares of the organization.

We many times will include these two objectives, because we found that considering these additional objectives in our competitor analysis often helps us better define a competitor's activities.

Chapter 3

Business Strategy

We assume that most organizations engage in some type of business strategy to meet their objectives. Common business strategies include:

- Protecting intellectual property. Getting a patent is a good example. This kind of action can prevent potential competitors from entering a market. For instance, a potential competitor probably won't enter a market if the competitor cannot get access to some necessary patented technology.

- Collaborating with other organizations through arrangements such as partnerships and joint ventures.

- Targeting a specific market or market segment.

- Making the market unstable. One of the ways to do this is to arbitrarily raise or lower prices.

- Investing in technology. This can be done by engaging in activities such as developing new technology, buying the license to technology, buying organizations with technology, and hiring people with technology knowledge.

We assume that an organization uses its strategic capability to achieve its objectives. We have therefore established a definition of, and measure for, strategic capability. We address this below.

STRATEGIC CAPABILITY

We define strategic capability as a measure of an organization's ability to set realistic objectives and use appropriate strategies to meet those objectives. A competitor is any one of the following five types of organizations: a direct rival, a buyer, a supplier, a possible entrant to your industry, or an organization that produces a substitute product or service for your product or service. And a competitor with high strategic capability is a competitor you want to monitor.

We assume that strategic capability is a function of the following four elements (Georgantzas and Acar 1995, 241):

- Management Capability

- Market Demand (or Access to Market Demand)

- Financial Resources (at the Organization's Disposal)

- Technology (the Ability to Use It Effectively, or Create It)

To estimate a competitor's strategic capability, the following questions, that reflect the generic objectives and strategies discussed above, should be asked and answered regarding the competitor. The more "yes" answers you get, the more strategically capable the competitor probably is. Here are the questions:

- Is there enough demand for the product or service to support the existing competitors?

- Is the organization making, or can it make an investment in technology?

- Is the organization making, or does it have the resources to make organization acquisitions?

- Is the organization forming, or does it have the potential to form alliances or engage in some type of collaboration?

- Is the organization bringing in, or can the organization bring in high-powered personnel or management talent?

- Is the organization influencing, or can the organization influence market demand using its marketing strength or technology strength?

IDENTIFYING STRATEGICALLY CAPABLE COMPETITORS

Identifying strategically capable competitors is very important for competitor analysis. We have developed two methods for performing this identification. The first method uses if-then rules based on strategically relevant articles, and the second method uses a sorting method based on competitor-related concepts. We discuss both of these methods below.

Chapter 3

Strategic Relevance

We devised a measure that can be automated, using text mining software, to indicate the likelihood that an article contains competitors with strategic capability. That measure is strategic relevance.

Strategic relevance is a measure of an article's competitor-related concepts within an industry domain. If certain keywords are found in an article, the article is considered to be strategically relevant. The organizations mentioned in the strategically relevant article are assumed likely to be strategically capable organizations. The types of keywords required to be in a strategically relevant article are called competitor-related keywords. The competitor-related keyword types chosen for use in this book's analysis are shown below.

Competitor-Related Keyword Types

We established seven competitor-related keyword types. The keyword types are as follows:

- An organization name indicator such as "inc.," "corp.," or "Corporation" [Type 1]

  These indicators signal the existence of an organization (probably a competitor) in the article.

- Different forms of the word "leader" [Type 2]

  This word, often, in a business article, indicates an organization that is very successful in a market.

- Some form of the word "market" [Type 3]

  This word, or some form of the word, typically signals something having to do with a product or service, the price of a product or service, the distribution of a product or service, the promotion of a product or service, market size, or something else having to do with the marketplace.

Competitor Analysis Techniques

- Technology words such as "research" and "development" [Type 4]

  These words, many times, signal a competitor's use or creation of some technology.

- Organization collaboration words such as "alliance" and "partnership" [Type 5]

  These words signal one or more organizations that are working with each other in some manner.

- Different forms of the words "merger" and "acquisition" [Type 6]

  These words signal organizations joining in a formal manner.

- Organization management titles such as "ceo" and "exec" [Type 7]

  These words signal organization management activity

Using If-then Rules to Identify Strategically Relevant Articles

In the first edition of this book, we introduced if-then rules as a way to identify articles that are likely to contain information about strategically capable organizations. We established the rules after manually examining many business articles. We implemented the rules in the text mining software discussed earlier. These rules use the competitor-related keyword types, mentioned in the last section, to select articles which are strategically relevant.

We assume that articles that are strategically relevant (they contain competitor-related keywords) probably contain competitor-related concepts. And we assume that some of the competitor-related concepts describe activities associated with strategically capable organizations.

The more competitor-related keyword types in an article, the more strategically capable, organizations mentioned in the article, are likely to be. To help us isolate the most important competitor-related concepts, our text mining software assigns a rating to each article based on the number of competitor-related keyword types in the article. We then analyze concepts from the highest rated articles.

The if-then rules are as follows:

- If an article contains a representative of each one of the seven competitor-related keyword types, or a reference to the word "patent," the article is given the highest strategic relevance rating of "1." (The word "patent" can possibly signal a strategically capable organization, so the word "patent" is given special weight.)

- If an article contains keyword representatives from any six of the seven competitor-related keyword types, the article is given a strategic relevance rating of "2."

- If an article contains keyword representatives from any five of the seven competitor-related keyword types, the article is given a strategic relevance rating of "3."

- If an article contains keyword representatives from any four of the seven competitor-related keyword types, the article is given a strategic relevance rating of "4."

- If an article contains keyword representatives from any three of the competitor-related keyword types, the article is given a strategic relevance rating of "5."

- If an article contains keyword representatives from any two of the competitor-related keyword types, or if an article contains an organization name indicator, the article is given a strategic relevance rating of "6." This is the lowest strategic relevance rating assigned to an article.

The more strategically relevant an article is, the more strategically capable are the organizations, mentioned in the article likely to be. To establish the strategic capability of a specific organization, the strategic capability-related questions mentioned above should be asked.

It should be noted that no article is ever associated with more than one relevance rating. After an article is selected for relevance and assigned the highest possible rating, that article is removed from the selection process.

Below, you will see concepts from articles identified using the above competitor-related if-then rules. All of the concepts contain keywords indicating organization names. Although we focus on concepts from strategically relevant articles containing organization name keywords, the if-then rules in our software can select relevant articles that contain no organization name keywords. Therefore, as part of our process, we also review strategically relevant articles containing no organization name keywords, to insure that we don't miss any important information.

Competitor Analysis Techniques

The competitor-related concepts and an identification number for each relevant article are part of the information written to files in the process outlined in figure 3.1 (this process was first shown in figure 1.7). The fifth rectangle (from the top) in the process flow indicates this information being written to files. The last rectangle in the flow describes opportunity and threat analysis that includes the competitor analysis.

Using a Sorting Method to Identify Strategically Capable Competitors

A few years after we wrote the first edition of this book, where we described our if-then method for identifying strategically capable competitors, we looked into simplifying that method. Toward that end, we decided to modify our text mining software to sort competitor-related concepts based on the number of keywords or phrases appearing in the concepts.

So instead of looking for articles containing the most competitor-related keywords, we started to look for competitor-related concepts containing the greatest number of environmental-forces keywords and phrases.

Over time, we found this method to be a simple and effective way to identify strategically capable competitors. Therefore, we adopted this method and generally use it in our analysis process. However, as we stated in the last section, the competitor-related concepts below were selected using the if-then rules described above.

Chapter 3

Text Mining and Business Analysis Process Flow

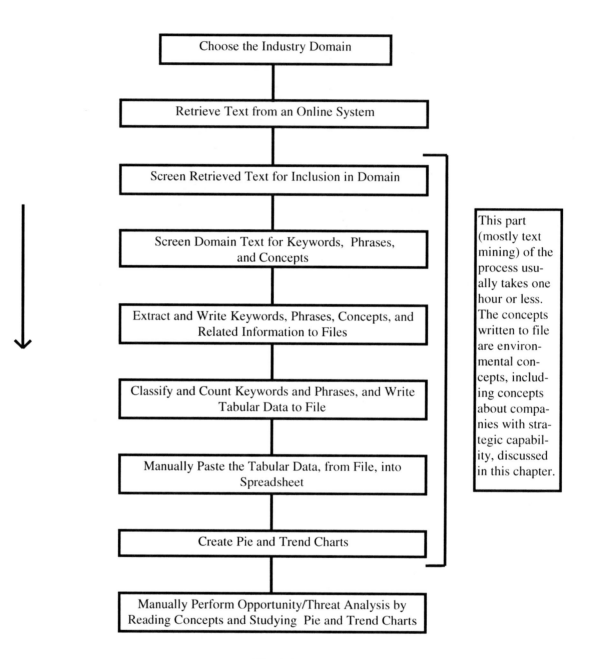

Fig. 3.1

CONCEPTS FOR STRATEGICALLY CAPABLE COMPETITORS

In a manner similar to the way concepts characterized environmental forces in chapter 2, the concepts in this section characterize the activities of competitors that may be strategically capable. Concepts for these competitors were identified in strategically relevant articles. The text mining software selected the relevant articles using the competitor-related if-then rules discussed above. The software then extracted the appropriate concepts. We show an actual concept (or keyword-excerpt) for a strategically capable organization in the air bag systems industry below:

Source: UPI
Date: January 8, 1991
Headline: Chrysler Introduces Minivan Air Bags with a Bang

"Chrysler Corp. demonstrated Tuesday the world's first public deployment of a driver's side air bag in a minivan, saying it will offer the safety device to . . . "

An air bag systems supplier would probably view the announcement in this concept as an opportunity. The supplier might contact Chrysler's air bag systems suppliers to ask about collaborative opportunities.

Concepts in this book are keyword-excerpts. But we don't show the actual competitor-related keyword-excerpts. We wanted to make the competitor-related concepts generic for our scenario and simulation analysis (chapter 6), so we paraphrased the competitor-related concepts and removed any organization names for our presentation in this book. (Paraphrasing the concepts and removing organization names is not a normal part of our text-mining and competitor analysis process.) A paraphrased version of the above UPI concept (keyword-excerpt), with the organization name removed, could read:

Competitor XYZ has become the first organization to publicly deploy a minivan driver's side air bag.

Below are the paraphrased versions of concepts describing the activities of strategically capable organizations. Twenty paraphrased concepts related to the air bag systems industry competitors (with actual organization names removed) are shown. The concepts were generated from articles with a strategic relevance rating of "3" or less. (The highest possible strategic relevance rating is "1.")

- **Concept 1:**   Competitor1 is one of the largest suppliers of air bag systems, and the organization has decided to split into two firms.

- **Concept 2:**   Competitor2 is one of the largest automobile manufacturers and it wants to be the first organization to offer air bags in its automobiles.

- **Concept 3**: Competitor3 is a supplier of the substance used to inflate air bags, and it wants to be the first U.S. supplier of the substance.

- **Concept 4**: Competitor4 is a joint venture supplying motorized seat belts that, at this time, are products which compete with air bags.

- **Concept 5**: Competitor5 is a large air bag systems component supplier and is raising $20 million with an Initial Public Offering (IPO).

- **Concept 6**: Competitor6 is an organization that will supply air bags to cars that didn't have air bags originally. The organization will offer retrofit air bags.

- **Concept 7**: Competitor7 is a large supplier of air bag systems, and this organization is going to start using computer air bag modeling in its air bag research.

- **Concept 8**: Competitor8, a large automobile manufacturer, expects to be using a new type of air bag system in its automobiles.

- **Concept 9**: Competitor9 is a supplier of air bag systems and will produce a low-cost air bag system.

- **Concept 10**: Competitor10 is a producer of air bag systems and is purchasing another air bag systems supplier.

- **Concept 11**: Competitor11 is a supplier and wants to be the first supplier to provide side air bags.

- **Concept 12**: Competitor12 is a supplier of air bag systems and is bringing in new personnel.

- **Concept 13**: Competitor13 is a supplier of air bag systems and will start producing reduced-size air bags.

- **Concept 14**: Competitor14 is a large automobile manufacturer and wants to be the first to offer rear seat air bag systems.

- **Concept 15**: Competitor15 has received a large contract to supply mini air bag systems.

- **Concept 16**: Competitor16 is an inventor who plans to develop safer, lower-priced air bag systems.

- **Concept 17**: Competitor17 is suing another competitor for royalties.

- **Concept 18**: Competitor18 is building new factories.

- **Concept 19**: Competitor19 is a direct rival (a fabric producer) that has made an agreement with another competitor (a supplier) to make advanced air bags.

- **Concept 20**: Competitor20 has developed a child seat to protect children from inflating air bags.

These concepts will be used for scenario and simulation analysis in chapter 6.

Chapter 3

SUMMARY

In this book, we use seven common business objectives to perform competitor analysis. And we assume that organizations are in business to do one or more of the following:

- Achieve Low-Price Position
- Specialize in a Market or Market Segment
- Sell the Top Quality Product or Service
- Achieve Vertical Integration
- Become the Technological Leader
- Obtain Brand Name Identification
- Become a Value Added Provider (or Add Service to the Product Line)

We noted in this chapter that for our day-to-day analysis methodology, we have added two more objectives to our list of common business objectives. These two objectives are "expand market" and "obtain capital."

Common business strategies that organizations use include:

- Taking steps to protect intellectual property—getting a patent, for example. This kind of action can prevent potential competitors from entering a market. For instance, a potential competitor that cannot get access to some necessary patented technology probably won't enter a market.
- Collaborating with other organizations through arrangements such as partnerships and joint ventures.
- Targeting a specific market or market segment.
- Making the market unstable. One of the ways to do this is to arbitrarily raise or lower prices.
- Investing in technology. This can be done by engaging in activities such as developing new technology, buying the license to technology, buying organizations with technology, and hiring people with technology knowledge.

We defined strategic capability as a measure of an organization's ability to set realistic objectives and use appropriate strategies to meet those objectives. A competitor is any one of the following five types of organizations: a direct rival, a buyer, a supplier, a possible entrant to your industry, or an organization that produces a substitute product or service for your product or service.

It is important to know which competitors have high strategic capability. We developed two methods to help identify these competitors. One method uses if-then rules and the other method uses a sorting approach. We implemented both of these methods in our text mining software. However, generally, we now use the sorting method to identify the most important strategically capable organizations.

Chapter 4   Environment and Competitor Analysis Methods

CHAPTER OVERVIEW

This chapter introduces our business information analysis methods that use forms as facilitators to help you determine or document dominant environmental forces, hone your organization's business objectives, ferret out your competitor's business objectives, and perform competitor analysis. The primary method used for competitor analysis is scenario and simulation. Once text mining methods have delivered the business concepts, the procedures introduced in this chapter can be used to help you convert the concepts into actions.

ENVIRONMENTAL FORCES ANALYSIS

As stated earlier, examining external forces for opportunities and threats is an important part of business information analysis. To aid in this analysis, the ENVIRONMENTAL FORCES FORM has been created to encourage you to think about your organization's environment. The form (figure 4.1) helps you determine which force at work in your business environment is likely to have the most effect on your organization's activities.

    As you can see, this form lists the same ten force types that we discussed in chapter 1. You are asked to choose the dominant force type for the industry under investigation by checking the appropriate box. To aid your thought process, the kinds of keywords that indicate a given force are shown in parentheses on the form.

Chapter 4

ENVIRONMENTAL FORCES FORM

ENVIRONMENTAL FORCES INDUSTRY:	INDICATE THE DOMINANT FORCE (S) WITH A CHECK MARK.
REGULATORY FORCES (regulation, regulate, regulatory)*	☐
LITIGATION FORCES (judge, suit, sue, legal, appellate, plaintiff, malpractice, indict)*	☐
POLITICAL FORCES (political, politics)*	☐
GOVERNMENTAL FORCES (government, federal, agenc, council, admin, Commission, senate, congress)*	☐
FOREIGN FORCES (foreign, Europe, international, export, import)*	☐
TECHNOLOGY FORCES (technolog, scien, engineer, developmental, design, develop, patent, research)*	☐
MANAGEMENT FORCES (ceo, manager, executive)*	☐
COLLABORATIVE FORCES (alliance, partnership, acquisition, merger)*	☐
COMPETITOR FORCES (rivals, suppliers, buyers, substitutes, potential entrants)*	☐
MARKET FORCES (marketing, marketplace)*	☐

*Note: The parentheses contain examples of words or roots of words we look for.

COMMENTS:

Fig. 4.1

BUSINESS OBJECTIVES ANALYSIS

It is paramount that you know what your organization's objectives are. To help you hone your understanding of your organization's objectives, a form entitled YOUR BUSINESS OBJECTIVES FORM (figure 4.2) was devised. We use this form to pinpoint business objectives. The form allows you to look at a set of general business objectives and choose the objective, or objectives, that best match your organization's real objectives.

Although it is possible to establish numerous business objectives, a set of seven objectives, first introduced in chapter 3, is used in this book and is listed (in slightly modified form) on the YOUR BUSINESS OBJECTIVES FORM in figure 4.2. Because it is so important to understand business objectives, we discuss them further below. For the exercises in this book, we assume that most organizations are in business to do one or more of the following:

- **Achieve Low-Price Position**

    This generally means that an organization wants its product or service to carry the lowest price when compared to the organization's competitors' product or service price. This is not considered by many business strategists to be a viable objective since it is very easy for an organization to retaliate, to another organization, by simply lowering its price. If both organizations continue to lower a product or service price in retaliation to each other, they could both lose money in the end.

- **Specialize in a Specific Market or Market Segment**

    This generally means that an organization has chosen a specific set of buyers to target. For example, you may tailor a product or service so that small businesses are likely to want to purchase the product or service. Or you may tailor your product or service for a specific demographic group and direct your advertising to that group.

- **Sell the Top Quality Product or Service**

    This generally means that an organization has chosen to aim for low product defects or service errors. The organization would probably put quality programs in place to catch errors and defects before the service or product gets to the customer.

- **Achieve a High Degree of Vertical Integration**

    This generally means that an organization will try to bring most of the production in-house and subcontract out as little as possible. Or, instead of giving its product to an outside sales group, for example, the organization might train its own sales force and sell its own product.

- **Become the Technological Leader**

    This generally means that an organization will invest heavily in research and development, or buy access to technology. The organization will try to become known for its technological innovations.

- **Obtain Brand Name Identification**

    This generally means that an organization will invest in activities that will let its market know about its product or service. Many times an organization will increase its investment in marketing to get the word out.

- **Become a Value Added Provider (or Add Service to the Product Line)**

    This generally means that an organization will try to add more value (usually more service) to its product or service. The organization will try to give a customer more for the money than its competitors, or at least appear to be doing so.

The YOUR BUSINESS OBJECTIVES FORM in figure 4.2 lists seven objectives and requests that you select the one that best matches your organization's business objectives. The above explanation of the objectives may help you better choose the appropriate objective (or objectives). Once this is done, the competitor analysis, which we discuss below, should begin.

Environment and Competitor Analysis Methods

YOUR BUSINESS OBJECTIVES FORM

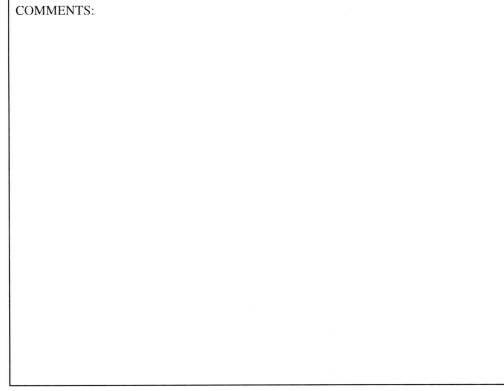

YOUR BUSINESS OBJECTIVES YOUR ORGANIZATION NAME: INDUSTRY:	INDICATE YOUR BUSINESS OB-JECTIVE(S) WITH A CHECK MARK.
To achieve low-price position	☐
To specialize in a market or market segment	☐
To sell the Top Quality Product/Service (Low product defect or low service error rate)	☐
To achieve vertical integration	☐
To be the technological leader	☐
To obtain brand identification	☐
To add service to product line	☐

COMMENTS:

Fig. 4.2

Chapter 4

COMPETITOR ANALYSIS

Once the environment has been analyzed, and an organization has clarified its objectives, competitor activities can perhaps be viewed from a more proper perspective. We devised three forms to aid in the understanding of a competitor (figure 4.3).

The first form in the figure is the COMPETITOR ACTIVITIES FORM that lets you describe your competitor's activities. On this form you simply state what you think the competitor is doing. The second form is the COMPETITOR BUSINESS OBJECTIVES FORM. The components of this form are identical to the components of the YOUR BUSINESS OBJECTIVES FORM (figure 4.2). The components were discussed above. The COMPETITOR BUSINESS OBJECTIVES FORM is used to allow you to assign an appropriate business objective (or set of objectives) to a competitor.

The last form in figure 4.3 is the STRATEGIC CAPABILITY FORM. This form makes it possible for you to approximate a competitor's strategic capability. Repeating what was stated in chapter 3, strategic capability is a measure of an organization's ability to set realistic objectives and to use appropriate strategies to meet the objectives. Strategic capability is a function of the following elements:

- Management Capability

- Market Demand (or Access to Market Demand)

- Financial Resources (at the Organization's Disposal)

- Technology (the Ability to Use It Effectively, or Create It)

A competitor having ample access to all four strategic capability elements may have superior strategic capability compared to your organization. That competitor may be able to use business tactics and strategies to threaten your organization. Therefore, based on what you can ascertain about a competitor, it is always in your best interest to make a best guess at a competitor's strategic capability.

To help you achieve this best guess, the STRATEGIC CAPABILITY FORM requires that you enter "1" or "0" for the following strategic capability questions:

- Is there enough demand for the product or service to support the existing competitors?

- Is the organization making, or can it make an investment in technology?

- Is the organization making, or does it have the resources to make organization acquisitions?

- Is the organization forming, or does it have the potential to form alliances or engage in some type of collaboration?

- Is the organization bringing in, or can the organization bring in high-powered personnel or management talent?

- Is the organization influencing, or can the organization influence market demand using its marketing strength or technology strength?

Once a "1" for "yes" or "0" for "no" is entered on the form, the numbers are totaled. (In practice, the line can be left blank to represent "0.") The total is your best guess of the competitor's strategic capability. The larger the total, the greater the assumed strategic capability of the competitor.

We would like to make one note here: The Strategic Capability Form can be used to analyze your organization, as well as a competitor's. So, if you need to determine how your organization stacks up against other organizations, use the Strategic Capability Form to do so.

Chapter 4

Competitor Analysis Forms

COMPETITOR ACTIVITIES FORM

What is the competitor doing?

COMPETITOR BUSINESS OBJECTIVES FORM

"COMPETITOR'S" BUSINESS OBJECTIVES INDUSTRY: COMPETITOR:	INDICATE COMPETITOR'S BUSINESS OBJECTIVE(S) WITH A CHECK MARK.
To achieve low-price position	☐
To specialize in a market or market segment	☐
To sell the Top Quality Product/Service (Low product defect or low service error rate)	☐
To achieve vertical integration	☐
To be the technological leader	☐
To obtain brand identification	☐
To add service to product line	☐

STRATEGIC CAPABILITY FORM

COMPETITOR STRATEGIC CAPABILITY PARAMETER ESTIMATION INDUSTRY: COMPETITOR:	INDICATE "1" FOR YES, OR "0" FOR NO.
Is there enough demand for the product or service to support the existing competitors?	
Is the organization making, or can it make an investment in technology?	
Is the organization making, or does it have the resources to make organization acquisitions?	
Is the organization forming, or does it have the potential to form alliances or engage in some type of collaboration?	
Is the organization bringing in, or can the organization bring in high-powered personnel or management talent?	
Is the organization influencing, or can the organization influence market demand using its marketing strength or technology strength?	
TOTAL (STRATEGIC CAPABILITY):	

Fig. 4.3

SCENARIO AND SIMULATION ANALYSIS

What Is a Scenario and What Is Simulation?

We define a scenario as an outline of plausible events. We define a simulation as an exercise where we act out (sometimes with the help of an outline or computer) the scenario events and their effects. Scenario and simulation analysis has been used in a number of areas for many years. Scenario and simulation analysis is used to train pilots, train surgeons, help establish business strategy, and plan space missions. For example, before a mission is flown by the space shuttle, NASA, using shuttle and environmental models, runs computer simulations assuming various scenarios. In some cases, the results are analyzed to determine the appropriate actions to be carried out during an upcoming mission.

Some of the scenarios and simulations are exercises where an analyst makes computer "runs" for his or her own purposes. And some of the scenarios and simulations are exercises consisting of a full-blown acting out of mission events. These full-blown scenarios and simulations put mission-critical computers and humans (flight controllers, engineers, managers, and other key people) "in the loop."

In chapter 6, scenarios and simulations are used in the development of business strategies. We, as analysts at **Mythical Air Bag Materials**, review the results of the air bag systems environmental text mining methods. We establish scenarios. We use simulations to analyze responses to scenario events. And we choose business strategies based on our scenario and simulation results.

Our Scenario and Simulation Method

We first establish a dominant environmental force. Establishing a dominant force enables us to determine conditions that usually accompany that force. Determining the accompanying conditions allows us to decide on a plausible, future environment for an organization.

Once we have chosen an environment, we use this environment to help us establish scenarios. After establishing the scenario, we use forms to promote simulation. Using forms makes a simulation very accessible, manual, and efficient. The simulation related forms are shown in figures 4.4 and 4.5. Figure 4.4 is the SIMULATION INITIALIZATION FORM. On this form, we initialize the simulation with environmental conditions, competitor information, and our most precise description of the competitor's objective.

The form requests the following:

- **Information about your industry's dominant environmental force or forces**

These are the forces that are most likely to affect your organization's success. We note on the form that these forces can be critical to an organization's success.

- **Information about your competitor's moves**

  Here, you describe your competitor's activities. This information might be found on the COMPETITOR ACTIVITIES FORM.

- **Information about your competitor's business objective(s)**

  Here, you attempt to identify your competitor's objective(s), based on its moves.

- **Information about your competitor's strategic capability**

  This input may have been indicated on the STRATEGIC CAPABILITY FORM. If so, get the total measurement from that form. If not, make a best guess at a competitor's strategic capability.

- **Information about your organization's business objectives**

  This is where you indicate your business objectives. Try to choose from the seven objectives discussed above.

- **The answer to this question: Does the dominant environmental force affect your competitor's objectives?**

  Here, you indicate your opinion of how the environmental forces will affect what you think are your competitor's business objectives.

- **The answer to this question: Does the dominant environmental force affect your objectives?**

  Here, of course, you should indicate whether the environmental forces will affect your organization's business objectives.

- **Your opinion of whether your competitor will notice your activities**

  For various reasons—your organization may be small for example—you may believe that you can make certain moves without any fear of being noticed by your competitor. If so, indicate that the competitor will not notice your moves. Otherwise, you should indicate that the competitor will notice.

- **Comments**

    In the comments section (figure 4.4), you can indicate anything you think might be appropriate.

    Figure 4.5 is the SIMULATION FORM. This form consists of five levels (A, B, C, D, E). These levels allow you to pretend that your competitor and your organization make certain moves. After the moves are made, you indicate what the response will be. This form is set up to assume that your competitor is the first actor. However, with a few modifications to the level titles, the form can be used to simulate activities that could occur if your organization initiates the series of moves. The levels are explained below:

Simulation Levels

- **Level A describes the competitor's move(s).**

    This is where you indicate the activity you assume the competitor is engaged in. This information might come from the COMPETITOR ACTIVITIES FORM, if you filled it out. If you did fill that form out, you should match the description of the competitor's activity to one of the nine items in Level A of the form. If you did not fill that form out, you can simply indicate what you think the competitor is doing or what the competitor's objective is. The nine items at Level A are a combination of the business objective items and the strategy items that we introduced in chapter 3.

- **Level B describes your response.**

    This is where you indicate your response to the competitor's move at Level A. There are twelve selectable items at Level B. Nine of the items are identical to the nine Level A items. The three additional selectable items in Level B give you a chance to do one of the following: simulate ignoring the competitor's last move, simulate accommodating or actually helping the competitor, or simulate your organization's exiting the market so that your organization does not have to compete with the competitor.

- **Level C describes the competitor's response.**

    This is where you indicate what you think the competitor's response will be, based on what you and the competitor have done so far, and on the objectives of your organization and the competitor. The number of selectable items is twelve, identical to those at Level B.

- **Level D describes your response.**

  This is where you, again, indicate your response to the competitor's last move. Here you must keep in mind all actions that have come before and all objectives that have been determined. The selectable items are identical to those at Levels B and C.

- **Level E describes your strategy to address the scenario and simulation.**

  This is where you choose a strategy for your organization. Here, you should take all moves (A through D) of your organization and your competitor into account.

  Finally, in figure 4.6 we show the FINAL STRATEGY FORM. This form requests that you choose a strategy that best captures your organization's response to one or more scenario situations.

SIMULATION INITIALIZATION FORM

COMPETITOR:
   INDUSTRY:

ASSUMPTIONS/KNOWLEDGE

Dominant Environmental Force(s) [Critical Success Factor(s)]:

Competitor's Move(s):

Precise Competitor's Business Objective(s):

Competitor's Strategic Capability (1-6, 6 being highest. Do scenario, if sc >= 3):
[Build scenarios for organizations with sc >=3]

Your Organization's Business Objective(s):

Does Dominant Environmental Force Affect Your Competitor's Objective(s)? (YES OR NO)

Does Dominant Environmental Force Affect Your Objective(s)? (YES OR NO)

Probability [HIGH/LOW] competitor will notice your moves:

COMMENTS:

Fig. 4.4

Chapter 4

SIMULATION FORM

SCENARIO 1 (Take into account the environmental forces):

A. Competitor's Move(s):

    Check each of the following that apply to indicate what the competitor is doing or will likely do:

    lower/raise price ☐   specialize in a market ☐   be quality leader ☐   increase vertical integration ☐

    increase investment in technology ☐   achieve brand name ☐   add services ☐   collaborate ☐

    increase investment in marketing ☐

    Comments:

B. Your Response:

    Check each of the following that apply to indicate what your response is:

    ignore ☐   accommodate ☐   exit the market ☐   lower/raise price ☐   specialize in a market ☐

    be quality leader ☐   increase vertical integration ☐   increase investment in technology ☐

    achieve brand name ☐   add services ☐   collaborate ☐   increase investment in marketing ☐

    Comments:

C. Competitor's Response:

    Check each of the following that apply to indicate what your competitor's response is:

    ignore ☐   accommodate ☐   exit the market ☐   lower/raise price ☐   specialize in a market ☐

    be quality leader ☐   increase vertical integration ☐   increase investment in technology ☐

    achieve brand name ☐   add services ☐   collaborate ☐   increase investment in marketing ☐

    Comments:

D. Your Response:

    Check each of the following that apply to indicate what your response is:

    ignore ☐   accommodate ☐   exit the market ☐   lower/raise price ☐   specialize in a market ☐

    be quality leader ☐   increase vertical integration ☐   increase investment in technology ☐

    achieve brand name ☐   add services ☐   collaborate ☐   increase investment in marketing ☐

E. Your strategy to address scenario:

Fig. 4.5

FINAL STRATEGY FORM

DATE: /   /

YOUR ORGANIZATION NAME:

DOMINANT FORCE (S):

COMPETITOR (S):

CHOSEN STRATEGY:

DOES THIS STRATEGY TAKE ADVANTAGE OF THE DOMINANT FORCE?   YES ☐   NO ☐

DOES THE DOMINANT FORCE THREATEN YOUR CHOSEN STRATEGY?   YES ☐   NO ☐

COMMENTS:

Fig. 4.6

STRATEGIC MANAGEMENT

As we said in chapter one, we see strategic management as the broader process of analyzing an organization's environment, establishing business objectives, and planning and engaging in activities to meet those objectives. Further, business intelligence is at the heart of strategic management. And the analysis methodology discussed above allows a strategic analyst to gain business intelligence. The analysis methodology enhances the analyst's ability to focus on important elements of strategic management. In the following chapters, we will demonstrate how you can use the methodology to improve a strategic position.

Chapter 4

SUMMARY

We use forms to facilitate the analysis of the environment and competitors. The ENVIRONMENTAL FORCES FORM is used to facilitate the analysis of the environment. Ten major environmental force types are listed on this form, and you are encouraged to choose your industry's dominant force type from one of the ten options. Using this form enables you to consider specific environmental forces in tactical and strategic planning.

Understanding and analyzing business objectives is an important part of business information analysis. For the exercises in this book, we assume that there are seven basic objectives from which most organizations choose when establishing their business goals. Two of our forms use these objectives as part of the competitor analysis. The first form is called the YOUR BUSINESS OBJECTIVES FORM. The second form is the COMPETITOR BUSINESS OBJECTIVES FORM. These two forms can help you understand your organization's business objectives and your competitor's business objectives.

We use three forms to facilitate the analysis of a competitor's moves. The first form is the COMPETITOR ACTIVITIES FORM which lets you describe a competitor's activities. On this form, you simply state what you think the competitor is doing. The second form is the COMPETITOR BUSINESS OBJECTIVES FORM mentioned above. The last of the three competitor analysis forms is the STRATEGIC CAPABILITY FORM. This form is used to enable you to make a best guess at a competitor's strategic capability.

Questions are asked on this form concerning a competitor's ability to set objectives and establish strategies to meet those objectives. If your answer is "yes" to a question on the form, a "1" should be entered on the form next to the question. If your answer to a question is "no," a "0" should be entered (or the line can be left blank) on the form next to the question. The numbers are then added to get an estimate of the competitor's strategic capability.

The SIMULATION FORM is a form that allows you to focus on a competitor's move(s). This form enables you to indicate your most strategically appropriate response(s) to a competitor's current and possible future move(s). The last form of the chapter is the FINAL STRATEGY FORM. This form prompts you to choose an appropriate business strategy for your organization that takes into account the results of all scenarios.

Chapter 5   Environment and Objectives Analysis Results

CHAPTER OVERVIEW

In the last chapter, we introduced you to specific analysis methods. In the current chapter, we use some of those analysis methods to assess real industry information. We use information from the air bag systems industry to fill out the ENVIRONMENTAL FORCES FORM. And we use **Mythical Air Bag Materials'** business objectives and **Mythical Air Bag Materials'** view of the air bags systems industry to fill out the YOUR BUSINESS OBJECTIVES FORM.

ENVIRONMENTAL FORCES AND YOUR BUSINESS OBJECTIVES

Figures 5.1 and 5.2 show a completed ENVIRONMENTAL FORCES FORM and a completed YOUR BUSINESS OBJECTIVES FORM, respectively. These forms are filled out from the perspective of our fictional organization, **Mythical Air Bag Materials**. Let's assume that our organization has been scanning air bag systems industry text for a few years, using text mining methods. And let's assume that we are performing this environmental forces analysis during the early 1990s.

During our analysis period, the GOVERNMENT was the dominant force, as shown in the environmental forces charts in chapter 2. So, the ENVIRONMENTAL FORCES FORM (figure 5.1) is filled out accordingly.

Chapter 5

Our Organization's Objective and Business Outlook

Mythical Air Bag Materials' main objective is to be a technological leader in the air bag fabric area. And we have a positive outlook for our future. We believe that the air bag inflatable component is one of the most important air bag system components. Further, we feel that the government, as the dominant force, will encourage technology advancements in air bag system components, including the inflatable component. Therefore, if **Mythical Air Bag Materials** can achieve the technological lead in air bag fabric production, we will enjoy a bright future. And becoming the technological leader is our objective, as shown in figure 5.2, by the "x" in the box for "**To be the technological leader.**"

Environment and Objectives Analysis Results

A Completed "ENVIRONMENTAL FORCES FORM" Example

ENVIRONMENTAL FORCES FORM

ENVIRONMENTAL FORCES INDUSTRY: Air Bag Systems (1989-1990)	INDICATE THE DOMI-NANT FORCE (S) WITH A CHECK MARK.
REGULATORY FORCES (regulation, regulate, regulatory)*	☐
LITIGATION FORCES (judge, suit, sue, legal, appellate, plaintiff, malpractice, in-dict)*	☐
POLITICAL FORCES (political, politics)*	☐
GOVERNMENTAL FORCES (government, federal, agenc, council, admin, Commis-sion, senate, congress)*	☒
FOREIGN FORCES (foreign, Europe, international, export, import)*	☐
TECHNOLOGY FORCES (technolog, scien, engineer, developmental, design, de-velop, patent, research)*	☐
MANAGEMENT FORCES (ceo, manager, executive)*	☐
COLLABORATIVE FORCES (alliance, partnership, acquisition, merger)*	☐
COMPETITOR FORCES (rivals, suppliers, buyers, substitutes, potential entrants)*	☐
MARKET FORCES (marketing, marketplace)*	☐

*Note: The parentheses contain examples of words or roots of words we look for.

COMMENTS: The government has just started mandating the use of passive restraint systems in automobiles.

Fig. 5.1

Chapter 5

A Completed "YOUR BUSINESS OBJECTIVES FORM" Example

YOUR BUSINESS OBJECTIVES FORM

YOUR BUSINESS OBJECTIVES YOUR ORGANIZATION NAME: Mythical Air Bag Materials INDUSTRY: Air Bag Systems	INDICATE YOUR BUSINESS OB-JECTIVE(S) WITH A CHECK MARK.
To achieve low-price position	☐
To specialize in a market or market segment	☐
To sell the Top Quality Product/Service (Low product defect or low service error rate)	☐
To achieve vertical integration	☐
To be the technological leader	☒
To obtain brand identification	☐
To add service to product line	☐

COMMENTS: Mythical Air Bag Materials is striving to be the technology leader in the design of air bag fabric.

Fig. 5.2

SUMMARY

We can assess real industry-environmental information using a form called the ENVIRONMENTAL FORCES FORM. And we can assess our organization's business objectives using a form called the YOUR BUSINESS OBJECTIVES FORM.

Using the results from our environmental forces analysis (chapter 2), we concluded that the dominant force in the air bag systems industry was government for most of the early nineties. Therefore, we filled out the ENVIRONMENTAL FORCES FORM accordingly. **Mythical Air Bag Materials'** primary business objective is to become the technological leader in the fabric area of the air bag systems industry. Therefore, we filled out the YOUR BUSINESS OBJECTIVES FORM for **Mythical Air Bag Materials** by checking the "To be the technological leader" objective.

Chapter 6   Scenario and Simulation Analysis

CHAPTER OVERVIEW

In this chapter we show how competitor concepts (which represent competitor activities), derived from text mining efforts, can efficiently and effectively be converted into business intelligence using scenario and manual simulation. As we said in chapter 4, we define a scenario as an outline of plausible events. We define a simulation as an exercise where we act out (with the help of an outline or computer) the scenario events and their effects. We analyze scenarios and simulations to convert concepts into intelligence.

The intelligence can be used to gain insight into what a competitor is doing (or trying to do) now, what the competitor might do, and what a competitor's activities might mean to our organization in the future. We can use this intelligence to determine what action we should take to improve our organization's competitive position.

CONCEPTS FOR STRATEGICALLY CAPABLE COMPETITORS

Below we show the generated concepts for strategically capable competitors (originally shown in chapter 3), whose actions motivated the scenarios shown on the pages of the current chapter. We generated the concepts from keyword-excerpts that were extracted from strategically relevant articles using the competitor-related if-then rules discussed in chapter 3. Each one of the articles from which a concept was generated received a strategic relevance rating of "3" or less.

The concepts below describe the activities of strategically capable competitors. We show concepts for twenty organizations. Although the concepts are motivated by real competitor activities, actual competitor names are not used. On pages following the concepts, we show the associated scenarios and simulations. Our process demonstrates how competitor concepts can be converted into actionable information using scenario and simulation analysis. The concepts are shown below.

Competitor Concepts

- **Concept 1:** Competitor1 is one of the largest suppliers of air bag systems, and the organization has decided to split into two firms.

- **Concept 2:** Competitor2 is one of the largest automobile manufacturers and it wants to be the first organization to offer air bags in its automobiles.

- **Concept 3:** Competitor3 is a supplier of the substance used to inflate air bags, and it wants to be the first U.S. supplier of the substance.

- **Concept 4:** Competitor4 is a joint venture supplying motorized seat belts that, at this time, are products which compete with air bags.

- **Concept 5:** Competitor5 is a large air bag systems component supplier and is raising $20 million with an Initial Public Offering (IPO).

- **Concept 6:** Competitor6 is an organization that will supply air bags to cars that didn't have air bags originally. The organization will offer retrofit air bags.

- **Concept 7:** Competitor7 is a large supplier of air bag systems, and this organization is going to start using computer air bag modeling in its air bag research.

- **Concept 8:** Competitor8, a large automobile manufacturer, expects to be using a new type of air bag system in its automobiles.

- **Concept 9:** Competitor9 is a supplier of air bag systems and will produce a low-cost air bag system.

- **Concept 10:** Competitor10 is a producer of air bag systems and is purchasing another air bag systems supplier.

- **Concept 11:** Competitor11 is a supplier and wants to be the first supplier to provide side air bags.

- **Concept 12:** Competitor12 is a supplier of air bag systems and is bringing in new personnel.

- **Concept 13**: Competitor13 is a supplier of air bag systems and will start producing reduced-size air bags.

- **Concept 14**: Competitor14 is a large automobile manufacturer and wants to be the first to offer rear seat air bag systems.

- **Concept 15**: Competitor15 has received a large contract to supply mini air bag systems.

- **Concept 16**: Competitor16 is an inventor who plans to develop safer, lower-priced air bag systems.

- **Concept 17**: Competitor17 is suing another competitor for royalties.

- **Concept 18**: Competitor18 is building new factories.

- **Concept 19**: Competitor19 is a direct rival (a fabric producer) that has made an agreement with another competitor (a supplier) to make advanced air bags.

- **Concept 20**: Competitor20 has developed a child seat to protect children from inflating air bags.

Competitor Information

Once competitor concepts have been identified and extracted, additional information may be needed to better establish the assumptions required for the scenario and simulation analysis. Sources for this additional information might include the competitor's Internet Web site, business directories such as Dun & Bradstreet's directories, the yellow pages, industry consultants, or industry experts. If you are unable to find additional information, but you want to proceed with a scenario and simulation exercise, make a guess at the necessary information needed, and proceed.

For this chapter's scenario-simulation exercises, assume that our organization has somehow obtained the required information needed for input to the scenario and simulation forms. Also, assume that **Mythical Air Bag Materials'** business objective is to be the technological leader in the air bag fabric area. Assume that **Mythical Air Bag Materials'** outlook for the air bag systems industry is positive. And assume that **Mythical Air Bag Materials** has a strategic capability rating of "5."

The competitor assumptions for the scenarios and simulations are shown in the introduction to each one of the scenario and simulation exercises. We assume, for example, that all competitors under investigation have good competitive intelligence departments. Therefore, the competitors are assumed to be aware of **Mythical Air Bag Materials'** actions. The introduction also contains some hint of what the final strategy might be for our organization. The introduction is written to give you some idea of how the scenario and simulation exercise will proceed.

SCENARIO AND SIMULATION PROCESS OVERVIEW

On the page after each scenario-simulation exercise introduction, you will find the first three forms of the scenario-simulation process. Basically these forms are competitor analysis forms. On these forms, you are encouraged to describe the competitor's activities, the competitor's business objectives, and provide an estimate of the competitor's strategic capability. (See the process flow in figure 6.1.)

After these three forms (the competitor analysis forms) are completed, the simulation is initialized using the SIMULATION INITIALIZATION FORM. On this form, you are requested to indicate your organization's objectives. You are also requested to indicate your assumptions about, and knowledge of, the environment and your competitor.

The simulation exercise is shown on the page following each SIMULATION INITIALIZATION FORM. In the simulation exercise, you are encouraged to imagine the competitive process. There are five levels to each simulation exercise. The "checkable" options at a given level are based on the business objectives and strategies that organizations commonly employ in their competitive activities. The first level, Level A, is where you choose the move that best matches your competitor's actual or imagined moves. We will commonly use the activity described in the concept to determine the option to check at this level. There are nine possible competitor moves to choose from at Level A.

Level B is where you choose a response to your competitor's move or moves. There are twelve possible moves to choose from at this level. Nine of the moves are identical to the nine possible moves at Level A. And there are an additional three possible moves at this level. The moves at Level C are identical to the moves at Level B. At Level C, you are asked to indicate how you believe the competitor will respond to your last move or moves at Level B.

Level D is identical to Level C. At Level D, you are asked to indicate how your organization would respond to the competitor's move, or moves, at Level C. Level E is where you choose a strategy that best captures your set of responses to your competitor's moves.

At the end of the twenty scenario-simulation exercises in this chapter, you are requested to choose a final strategy, using the FINAL STRATEGY FORM, that best manages the opportunities and threats uncovered in the individual scenario-simulation exercises.

Chapter 6

Scenario-Simulation Process Flow

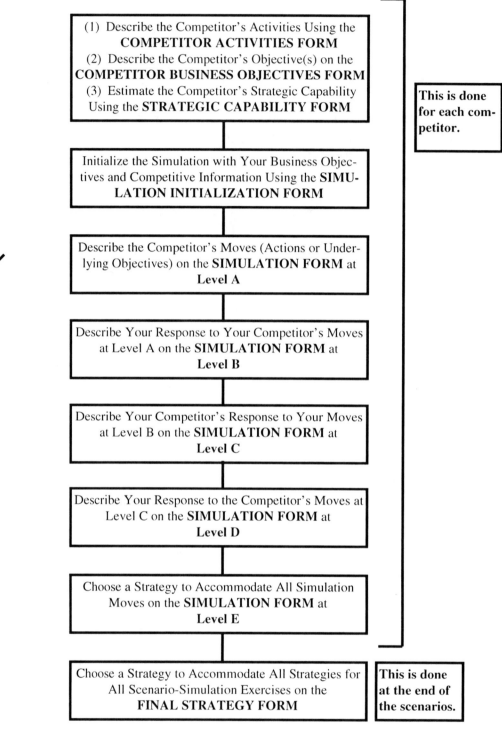

(1) Describe the Competitor's Activities Using the **COMPETITOR ACTIVITIES FORM**
(2) Describe the Competitor's Objective(s) on the **COMPETITOR BUSINESS OBJECTIVES FORM**
(3) Estimate the Competitor's Strategic Capability Using the **STRATEGIC CAPABILITY FORM**

Initialize the Simulation with Your Business Objectives and Competitive Information Using the **SIMU-LATION INITIALIZATION FORM**

Describe the Competitor's Moves (Actions or Under-lying Objectives) on the **SIMULATION FORM** at **Level A**

Describe Your Response to Your Competitor's Moves at Level A on the **SIMULATION FORM** at **Level B**

Describe Your Competitor's Response to Your Moves at Level B on the **SIMULATION FORM** at **Level C**

Describe Your Response to the Competitor's Moves at Level C on the **SIMULATION FORM** at **Level D**

Choose a Strategy to Accommodate All Simulation Moves on the **SIMULATION FORM** at **Level E**

This is done for each com-petitor.

Choose a Strategy to Accommodate All Strategies for All Scenario-Simulation Exercises on the **FINAL STRATEGY FORM**

This is done at the end of the scenarios.

Fig. 6.1

COMMENTS ON THE SCENARIOS AND SIMULATIONS

The scenarios and simulations are shown on the following pages. The first scenario is taken from Competitor Concept 1, the second scenario is taken from Competitor Concept 2, the third scenario is taken from Competitor Concept 3, and so on. These scenario examples are motivated by real-world (late 1989 through the early 1990s) air bag systems industry situations.

During this period in the air bag systems industry, the government was the dominant force. Also, during this period, a government mandate was in place requiring that new automobiles be equipped with passive restraint systems, including air bags and motorized seat belts.

In the following scenario-simulation exercises, the government is shown as the dominant force. And the force, for the most part, is positive for the air bag systems industry. For example, we would expect the government to monitor the technology associated with air bags, causing the technology to be improved. Also, because of the mandate mentioned above, we would expect a large market for air bag related equipment. Therefore, the government would create a positive environment for the air bag industry.

Chapter 6

SCENARIO 1: A Splitting Firm

Introduction: From Concept 1 above, we see that Competitor1 is one of the largest suppliers of air bag systems, and the organization has decided to split into two firms. Assumptions and knowledge about this competitor are as follows:

- This organization is splitting up so that one of the resulting organizations can focus on (or specialize in) air bag systems.

- This organization thinks that there is a lot of money to be made in the air bag systems industry.

- This organization has a relatively high strategic capability.

- This organization will notice our strategic moves.

- Only one of the new organizations (resulting from the split) will make air bag systems components.

If the derived air bag systems industry organization is going to focus on air bag systems, our organization should determine if the derived air bag systems organization presents a threat to our organization. This would be the case if the organization makes air bag fabric, or contracts with our direct competitors that make air bag fabric. No matter what, though, if our fabric is of the highest quality, we may be able to get a contract to supply air bag fabric to the new organization.

Using the results of our environmental forces analysis, our analysis of **Mythical Air Bag Materials'** business objectives in chapter 5, and the comments above, we will now complete our scenario and simulation analysis for Competitor1. (For this and all remaining scenario-simulation exercises, Levels B and D are **Mythical Air Bag Materials'** responses.)

Based on the above assumptions, we chose "specialize in a market" as the most likely objective Competitor1 is trying to meet. The appropriate items are checked on the following scenario-simulation analysis pages indicating this objective.

Scenario and Simulation Analysis

SCENARIO 1

COMPETITOR ACTIVITIES FORM

What is the competitor doing? Splitting into two firms

COMPETITOR BUSINESS OBJECTIVES FORM

"COMPETITOR'S" BUSINESS OBJECTIVES INDUSTRY: AIR BAG SYSTEMS COMPETITOR: Competitor1 (supplier)	INDICATE COMPETITOR'S BUSINESS OBJECTIVE(S) WITH A CHECK MARK.
To achieve low-price position	☐
To specialize in a market or market segment	☒
To sell the Top Quality Product/Service (Low product defect or low service error rate)	☐
To achieve vertical integration	☐
To be the technological leader	☐
To obtain brand identification	☐
To add service to product line	☐

STRATEGIC CAPABILITY FORM

COMPETITOR STRATEGIC CAPABILITY PARAMETER ESTIMATION INDUSTRY: AIR BAG SYSTEMS COMPETITOR: Competitor1	INDICATE "1" FOR YES, OR "0" FOR NO.
Is there enough demand for the product or service to support the existing competitors?	1
Is the organization making, or can it make an investment in technology?	1
Is the organization making, or does it have the resources to make organization acquisitions?	
Is the organization forming, or does it have the potential to form alliances or engage in some type of collaboration?	1
Is the organization bringing in, or can the organization bring in high-powered personnel or management talent?	
Is the organization influencing, or can the organization influence market demand using its marketing strength or technology strength?	1
TOTAL (STRATEGIC CAPABILITY):	4

Fig. 6.2

Chapter 6

SIMULATION INITIALIZATION FORM

COMPETITOR: Competitor1
    INDUSTRY: AIR BAG SYSTEMS

ASSUMPTIONS/KNOWLEDGE

Dominant Environmental Force(s) [Critical Success Factor(s)]: **Government**

Competitor's Move(s): **Splitting into 2 Firms**

Precise Competitor's Business Objective(s): **Allow One Organization to Specialize in Air Bag Systems**

Competitor's Strategic Capability (1-6, 6 being highest. Do scenario, if sc >= 3): **4**
[Build scenarios for organizations with sc >=3]

Your Organization's Business Objective(s): **To Be Technological Leader in Air Bag Fabrics**

Does Dominant Environmental Force Affect Your Competitor's Objective(s)? (YES OR NO) **YES**

Does Dominant Environmental Force Affect Your Objective(s)? (YES OR NO) **YES**

Probability [HIGH/LOW] competitor will notice your moves: **HIGH**

COMMENTS: Assume that Mythical Air Bag Materials has a strategic capability rating of "5." The only question on the Strategic Capability form that Mythical Air Bag Materials received a "0" on was the following: "Is the organization making, or does it have the resources to make organization acquisitions?" And we will assume that Mythical Air Bag Materials can effectively respond to Competitor1's actions.

Fig. 6.3

Scenario and Simulation Analysis

SCENARIO 1 (continued)   **[SIMULATION FORM]**

(Take into account the environmental forces)

A. Competitor's Move(s):

Check each of the following that apply to indicate what the competitor is doing or will likely do:

lower/raise price ☐ specialize in a market ☒ be quality leader ☐ increase vertical integration ☐

increase investment in technology ☐ achieve brand name ☐ add services ☐ collaborate ☐

increase investment in marketing ☐

Comments: **We have learned that this competitor will not currently make fabric.**

B. Your Response:

Check each of the following that apply to indicate what your response is:

ignore ☐ accommodate ☐ exit the market ☐ lower/raise price ☐ specialize in a market ☐

be quality leader ☐ increase vertical integration ☐ increase investment in technology ☒

achieve brand name ☐ add services ☐ collaborate ☐ increase investment in marketing ☒

Comments: **It may be a good idea to give the competitor a call.**

C. Competitor's Response:

Check each of the following that apply to indicate what your competitor's response is:

ignore ☒ accommodate ☐ exit the market ☐ lower/raise price ☐ specialize in a market ☐

be quality leader ☐ increase vertical integration ☐ increase investment in technology ☐

achieve brand name ☐ add services ☐ collaborate ☐ increase investment in marketing ☐

Comments: **Since Competitor1 is not making fabric, the competitor might ignore our organization.**

D. Your Response:

Check each of the following that apply to indicate what your response is:

ignore ☐ accommodate ☐ exit the market ☐ lower/raise price ☐ specialize in a market ☐

be quality leader ☐ increase vertical integration ☐ increase investment in technology ☒

achieve brand name ☐ add services ☐ collaborate ☒ increase investment in marketing ☐

E. Your strategy to address scenario: **Increase investment in technology, monitor competitor to determine if they will be making air bag fabrics, and look for collaborative opportunities.**

Fig. 6.4

133

Chapter 6

SCENARIO 2: First to Offer Air Bags

Introduction: From Concept 2 above, we see that Competitor2 is one of the largest automobile manufacturers, and the competitor wants to be the first organization to offer air bags in its automobiles. Assumptions and knowledge for this competitor are as follows:

- This organization is investing in technology.

- This organization is collaborating with other organizations.

- This organization wants to sell the safest automobiles.

- We take "safest" as a quality measure.

- This organization has high strategic capability.

- This organization will notice our moves.

Our organization should try to collaborate with the potential air bag system suppliers for this manufacturer. If we can impress this manufacturer's suppliers with our fabric, this will represent an opportunity. If not, it will represent a threat.

Using the results of our environmental forces analysis, our analysis of **Mythical Air Bag Materials'** business objectives in chapter 5, and the comments above, we now complete our scenario and simulation analysis for Competitor2.

Based on the above assumptions, we assumed that Competitor2 wants customers to view air bags as a quality feature for its automobiles. Therefore, we checked the quality related items for this competitor's objective where appropriate on the next three scenario-simulation pages. Other items are also checked on the simulation form (figure 6.7) that support our knowledge of the competitor.

Scenario and Simulation Analysis

SCENARIO 2

COMPETITOR ACTIVITIES FORM

What is the competitor doing? Trying to be the first organization to offer air bag systems in its automobiles

COMPETITOR BUSINESS OBJECTIVES FORM

"COMPETITOR'S" BUSINESS OBJECTIVES INDUSTRY: AIR BAG SYSTEMS COMPETITOR: Competitor2 (buyer)	INDICATE COMPETITOR'S BUSINESS OBJECTIVE(S) WITH A CHECK MARK.
To achieve low-price position	☐
To specialize in a market or market segment	☐
To sell the Top Quality Product/Service (Low product defect or low service error rate)	☒
To achieve vertical integration	☐
To be the technological leader	☐
To obtain brand identification	☐
To add service to product line	☐

STRATEGIC CAPABILITY FORM

COMPETITOR STRATEGIC CAPABILITY PARAMETER ESTIMATION INDUSTRY: AIR BAG SYSTEMS COMPETITOR: Competitor2	INDICATE "1" FOR YES, OR "0" FOR NO.
Is there enough demand for the product or service to support the existing competitors?	1
Is the organization making, or can it make an investment in technology?	1
Is the organization making, or does it have the resources to make organization acquisitions?	1
Is the organization forming, or does it have the potential to form alliances or engage in some type of collaboration?	1
Is the organization bringing in, or can the organization bring in high-powered personnel or management talent?	1
Is the organization influencing, or can the organization influence market demand using its marketing strength or technology strength?	1
TOTAL (STRATEGIC CAPABILITY):	6

Fig. 6.5

135

Chapter 6

SCENARIO 2 (continued)

SIMULATION INITIALIZATION FORM

COMPETITOR: Competitor2
    INDUSTRY: AIR BAG SYSTEMS

ASSUMPTIONS/KNOWLEDGE

Dominant Environmental Force(s) [Critical Success Factor(s)]: **Government**

Competitor's Move(s): **Adding Air Bags to Its Cars**

Precise Competitor's Business Objective(s): **Sell Safest Automobiles**

Competitor's Strategic Capability (1-6, 6 being highest. Do scenario, if sc >= 3): **6**
[Build scenarios for organizations with sc >=3]

Your Organization's Business Objective(s): **To Be Technological Leader**

Does Dominant Environmental Force Affect Your Competitor's Objective(s)? (YES OR NO) **YES**

Does Dominant Environmental Force Affect Your Objective(s)? (YES OR NO) **YES**

Probability [HIGH/LOW] competitor will notice your moves: **HIGH**

COMMENTS: Assume that Mythical Air Bag Materials has a strategic capability rating of "5." The only question on the Strategic Capability form that Mythical Air Bag Materials received a "0" on was the following: "Is the organization making, or does it have the resources to make organization acquisitions?" And we will assume that Mythical Air Bag Materials can effectively respond to Competitor2's actions.

Fig. 6.6

Scenario and Simulation Analysis

SCENARIO 2 (continued)   **[SIMULATION FORM]**

(Take into account the environmental forces)

A. Competitor's Move(s):

Check each of the following that apply to indicate what the competitor is doing or will likely do:

lower/raise price ☐ specialize in a market ☐ be quality leader ☒ increase vertical integration ☐

increase investment in technology ☒ achieve brand name ☐ add services ☐ collaborate ☒

increase investment in marketing ☐

Comments: **This is not a direct-rival situation, but this may be a collaborative opportunity.**

B. Your Response:

Check each of the following that apply to indicate what your response is:

ignore ☐ accommodate ☐ exit the market ☐ lower/raise price ☐ specialize in a market ☐

be quality leader ☐ increase vertical integration ☐ increase investment in technology ☒

achieve brand name ☐ add services ☐ collaborate ☒ increase investment in marketing ☐

Comments:

C. Competitor's Response:

Check each of the following that apply to indicate what your competitor's response is:

ignore ☐ accommodate ☐ exit the market ☐ lower/raise price ☐ specialize in a market ☐

be quality leader ☒ increase vertical integration ☐ increase investment in technology ☐

achieve brand name ☐ add services ☐ collaborate ☒ increase investment in marketing ☐

Comments:

D. Your Response:

Check each of the following that apply to indicate what your response is:

ignore ☐ accommodate ☐ exit the market ☐ lower/raise price ☐ specialize in a market ☐

be quality leader ☐ increase vertical integration ☐ increase investment in technology ☒

achieve brand name ☐ add services ☐ collaborate ☒ increase investment in marketing ☐

E. Your strategy to address scenario: **Increase investment in technology and monitor for collaborative opportunities.**

Fig. 6.7

137

Chapter 6

SCENARIO 3: First to Offer Air Bag Substance

Introduction: From Concept 3 above, we see that Competitor3 is a supplier of the major substance used to inflate air bags, and wants to be the first U.S. supplier. Assumptions and knowledge for this competitor are as follows:

- This organization has sold the substance in Canada.

- This organization sees the U.S. market as a potentially lucrative market for its substance.

- This organization has a relatively high strategic capability.

- This organization will specialize in the U.S. air bag substance market.

- This organization will notice our moves.

We want to try to collaborate with Competitor3 to see if we can get the organization to use our air bag fabric in testing. Using the results of our environmental forces analysis, our analysis of **Mythical Air Bag Materials'** business objectives in chapter 5, and the comments above, we now complete our scenario and simulation analysis for Competitor3. The next three pages show the analysis.

Based on the above assumptions, we concluded that Competitor3 wants to establish its name in the U.S. Therefore, on the following three scenario-simulation pages, the appropriate items that support this objective are checked.

Scenario and Simulation Analysis

SCENARIO 3

COMPETITOR ACTIVITIES FORM

What is the competitor doing? Competitor3 wants to become the first U. S. manufacturer of substance used to inflate air bags

COMPETITOR BUSINESS OBJECTIVES FORM

"COMPETITOR'S" BUSINESS OBJECTIVES INDUSTRY: AIR BAG SYSTEMS COMPETITOR: Competitor3 (supplier)	INDICATE COMPETITOR'S BUSINESS OBJECTIVE(S) WITH A CHECK MARK.
To achieve low-price position	☐
To specialize in a market or market segment	☐
To sell the Top Quality Product/Service (Low product defect or low service error rate)	☐
To achieve vertical integration	☐
To be the technological leader	☐
To obtain brand identification	☒
To add service to product line	☐

STRATEGIC CAPABILITY FORM

COMPETITOR STRATEGIC CAPABILITY PARAMETER ESTIMATION INDUSTRY: AIR BAG SYSTEMS COMPETITOR: Competitor3	INDICATE "1" FOR YES, OR "0" FOR NO.
Is there enough demand for the product or service to support the existing competitors?	1
Is the organization making, or can it make an investment in technology?	1
Is the organization making, or does it have the resources to make organization acquisitions?	
Is the organization forming, or does it have the potential to form alliances or engage in some type of collaboration?	
Is the organization bringing in, or can the organization bring in high-powered personnel or management talent?	
Is the organization influencing, or can the organization influence market demand using its marketing strength or technology strength?	1
TOTAL (STRATEGIC CAPABILITY):	3

Fig. 6.8

SCENARIO 3 (continued)

SIMULATION INITIALIZATION FORM

COMPETITOR: Competitor3
    INDUSTRY: AIR BAG SYSTEMS

ASSUMPTIONS/KNOWLEDGE

Dominant Environmental Force(s) [Critical Success Factor(s)]: **Government**

Competitor's Move(s): **Entering the Air Bag Market**

Precise Competitor's Business Objective(s): **Achieve Air Bag Substance Brand Name I.D. in U.S.**

Competitor's Strategic Capability (1-6, 6 being highest. Do scenario, if sc >= 3): **3**
[Build scenarios for organizations with sc >=3]

Your Organization's Business Objective(s): **To Be Technological Leader in Air Bag Fabrics**

Does Dominant Environmental Force Affect Your Competitor's Objective(s)? (YES OR NO) **YES**

Does Dominant Environmental Force Affect Your Objective(s)? (YES OR NO) **YES**

Probability [HIGH/LOW] competitor will notice your moves: **HIGH**

COMMENTS: Assume that Mythical Air Bag Materials has a strategic capability rating of "5." The only question on the Strategic Capability form that Mythical Air Bag Materials received a "0" on was the following: "Is the organization making, or does it have the resources to make organization acquisitions?" And we will assume that Mythical Air Bag Materials can effectively respond to Competitor3's actions.

Fig. 6.9

Scenario and Simulation Analysis

SCENARIO 3 (continued)   **[SIMULATION FORM]**

(Take into account the environmental forces)

A. Competitor's Move(s):

Check each of the following that apply to indicate what the competitor is doing or will likely do:

lower/raise price ☐ specialize in a market ☐ be quality leader ☐ increase vertical integration ☐

increase investment in technology ☐ achieve brand name ☒ add services ☐ collaborate ☐

increase investment in marketing ☐

Comments:

B. Your Response:

Check each of the following that apply to indicate what your response is:

ignore ☐ accommodate ☐ exit the market ☐ lower/raise price ☐ specialize in a market ☐

be quality leader ☐ increase vertical integration ☐ increase investment in technology ☒

achieve brand name ☐ add services ☐ collaborate ☐ increase investment in marketing ☐

Comments:

C. Competitor's Response:

Check each of the following that apply to indicate what your competitor's response is:

ignore ☐ accommodate ☐ exit the market ☐ lower/raise price ☐ specialize in a market ☐

be quality leader ☐ increase vertical integration ☐ increase investment in technology ☐

achieve brand name ☒ add services ☐ collaborate ☒ increase investment in marketing ☐

Comments: **This organization might try to collaborate with us and others in the air bag industry.**

D. Your Response:

Check each of the following that apply to indicate what your response is:

ignore ☐ accommodate ☐ exit the market ☐ lower/raise price ☐ specialize in a market ☐

be quality leader ☐ increase vertical integration ☐ increase investment in technology ☒

achieve brand name ☐ add services ☐ collaborate ☒ increase investment in marketing ☐

E. Your strategy to address scenario: **Increase investment in technology, look for collaborative opportunities.**

Fig. 6.10

Chapter 6

SCENARIO 4: Motorized Seat Belts

Introduction: From Concept 4 above, we see that Competitor4 is a joint venture supplying motorized seat belts that at this time are a product competing with air bags. Assumptions and knowledge for Competitor4 are as follows:

- This organization is using leverage to increase its capability.

- This organization is trying to make its name known in the industry.

- This organization has a relatively high strategic capability.

- This organization will notice our moves.

Our organization will need to monitor this organization and the government. Using the results of our environmental forces analysis, our analysis of our **Mythical Air Bag Materials'** business objectives in chapter 5, and the comments above, we now complete our scenario and simulation analysis for Competitor4.

Based on the assumptions above, we decided that Competitor4 wants to achieve brand name identification in the seat belt market. Therefore, the appropriate items reflecting this objective are checked on the next three scenario-simulation pages.

SCENARIO 4

COMPETITOR ACTIVITIES FORM

What is the competitor doing? Producing motorized seat belts

COMPETITOR BUSINESS OBJECTIVES FORM

"COMPETITOR'S" BUSINESS OBJECTIVES INDUSTRY: AIR BAG SYSTEMS COMPETITOR: Competitor4 (substitute)	INDICATE COMPETITOR'S BUSINESS OBJECTIVE(S) WITH A CHECK MARK.
To achieve low-price position	☐
To specialize in a market or market segment	☐
To sell the Top Quality Product/Service (Low product defect or low service error rate)	☐
To achieve vertical integration	☐
To be the technological leader	☐
To obtain brand identification	☒
To add service to product line	☐

STRATEGIC CAPABILITY FORM

COMPETITOR STRATEGIC CAPABILITY PARAMETER ESTIMATION INDUSTRY: AIR BAG SYSTEMS COMPETITOR: Competitor4	INDICATE "1" FOR YES, OR "0" FOR NO.
Is there enough demand for the product or service to support the existing competitors?	1
Is the organization making, or can it make an investment in technology?	
Is the organization making, or does it have the resources to make organization acquisitions?	
Is the organization forming, or does it have the potential to form alliances or engage in some type of collaboration?	1
Is the organization bringing in, or can the organization bring in high-powered personnel or management talent?	
Is the organization influencing, or can the organization influence market demand using its marketing strength or technology strength?	1
TOTAL (STRATEGIC CAPABILITY):	3

Fig. 6.11

Chapter 6

SIMULATION INITIALIZATION FORM

COMPETITOR: Competitor4
  INDUSTRY: AIR BAG SYSTEMS

ASSUMPTIONS/KNOWLEDGE

Dominant Environmental Force(s) [Critical Success Factor(s)]: **Government**

Competitor's Move(s): **Entering Passive/Active Auto Safety Market (Motorized Seat Belts)**

Precise Competitor's Business Objective(s): **To Obtain Motorized Seat Belt Brand Name Identification**

Competitor's Strategic Capability (1-6, 6 being highest. Do scenario, if sc >= 3): **3**
[Build scenarios for organizations with sc >=3]

Your Organization's Business Objective(s): **To Be Technological Leader in Air Bag Fabrics**

Does Dominant Environmental Force Affect Your Competitor's Objective(s)? (YES OR NO) **YES**

Does Dominant Environmental Force Affect Your Objective(s)? (YES OR NO) **YES**

Probability [HIGH/LOW] competitor will notice your moves: **HIGH**

COMMENTS: Assume that Mythical Air Bag Materials has a strategic capability rating of "5." The only question on the Strategic Capability form that Mythical Air Bag Materials received a "0" on was the following: "Is the organization making, or does it have the resources to make organization acquisitions?" And we will assume that Mythical Air Bag Materials can effectively respond to Competitor4's actions.

Fig. 6.12

Scenario and Simulation Analysis

SCENARIO 4 (continued)   **[SIMULATION FORM]**

(Take into account the environmental forces)

A. Competitor's Move(s):

Check each of the following that apply to indicate what the competitor is doing or will likely do:

lower/raise price ☐ specialize in a market ☐ be quality leader ☐ increase vertical integration ☐

increase investment in technology ☐ achieve brand name ☒ add services ☐ collaborate ☐

increase investment in marketing ☐

Comments: **Competitor4 wants to be *the* passive restraint system provider.**

B. Your Response:

Check each of the following that apply to indicate what your response is:

ignore ☐ accommodate ☐ exit the market ☐ lower/raise price ☐ specialize in a market ☐

be quality leader ☐ increase vertical integration ☐ increase investment in technology ☒

achieve brand name ☐ add services ☐ collaborate ☐ increase investment in marketing ☐

Comments: **Monitor the possible substitute.**

C. Competitor's Response:

Check each of the following that apply to indicate what your competitor's response is:

ignore ☒ accommodate ☐ exit the market ☐ lower/raise price ☐ specialize in a market ☐

be quality leader ☐ increase vertical integration ☐ increase investment in technology ☒

achieve brand name ☒ add services ☐ collaborate ☐ increase investment in marketing ☐

Comments:

D. Your Response:

Check each of the following that apply to indicate what your response is:

ignore ☐ accommodate ☐ exit the market ☐ lower/raise price ☐ specialize in a market ☐

be quality leader ☐ increase vertical integration ☐ increase investment in technology ☒

achieve brand name ☐ add services ☐ collaborate ☐ increase investment in marketing ☒

E. Your strategy to address scenario: **Increase tech investment; monitor competitor; monitor government regulations to determine what new regulations might be put in place.**

Fig. 6.13

Chapter 6

SCENARIO 5: Raising $20 Million

Introduction: From Concept 5 above, we see that Competitor5 is a large air bag component supplier and the organization is raising $20 million with an Initial Public Offering (IPO). Assumptions and knowledge for this competitor are as follows:

- This organization is raising money to invest in technology.

- This organization is raising money to invest in more marketing.

- This organization has a relatively high strategic capability.

- This organization will notice our moves.

Our organization needs to make sure we have some idea of the direction this competitor will take. This organization does not make air bag fabrics. Still, since the components this organization makes interact with our fabric, we need to make sure we know what this organization is doing, or might do, strategically.

Using the results of our environmental forces analysis, our analysis of **Mythical Air Bag Materials** business objectives in chapter 5, and the comments above, we now complete our scenario and simulation analysis for Competitor5. Based on the assumptions, we concluded that Competitor5 is trying to raise money to invest in technology and marketing. Therefore, appropriate items are checked on the following three scenario-simulation pages to support these objectives.

Technology is assumed to be the main competitor objective, while marketing is assumed to be a sub-objective. Therefore, "Invest in Technology" is shown as the competitor's objective (figure 6.15). Technology is checked on the simulation form (figure 6.16), along with the competitor's apparent desire to increase its investment in marketing.

Scenario and Simulation Analysis

SCENARIO 5

COMPETITOR ACTIVITIES FORM

What is the competitor doing? Component maker raising $20 million with Initial Public Offering (IPO)

COMPETITOR BUSINESS OBJECTIVES FORM

"COMPETITOR'S" BUSINESS OBJECTIVES INDUSTRY: AIR BAG SYSTEMS COMPETITOR: Competitor5 (supplier)	INDICATE COMPETITOR'S BUSINESS OBJECTIVE(S) WITH A CHECK MARK.
To achieve low-price position	☐
To specialize in a market or market segment	☐
To sell the Top Quality Product/Service (Low product defect or low service error rate)	☐
To achieve vertical integration	☐
To be the technological leader	☒
To obtain brand identification	☐
To add service to product line	☐

STRATEGIC CAPABILITY FORM

COMPETITOR STRATEGIC CAPABILITY PARAMETER ESTIMATION INDUSTRY: AIR BAG SYSTEMS COMPETITOR: Competitor5	INDICATE "1" FOR YES, OR "0" FOR NO.
Is there enough demand for the product or service to support the existing competitors?	1
Is the organization making, or can it make an investment in technology?	1
Is the organization making, or does it have the resources to make organization acquisitions?	
Is the organization forming, or does it have the potential to form alliances or engage in some type of collaboration?	
Is the organization bringing in, or can the organization bring in high-powered personnel or management talent?	1
Is the organization influencing, or can the organization influence market demand using its marketing strength or technology strength?	
TOTAL (STRATEGIC CAPABILITY):	**3**

Fig. 6.14

Chapter 6

SIMULATION INITIALIZATION FORM

COMPETITOR: Competitor5
   INDUSTRY: AIR BAG SYSTEMS

ASSUMPTIONS/KNOWLEDGE

Dominant Environmental Force(s) [Critical Success Factor(s)]: **Government**

Competitor's Move(s): **Raising $20 Million with IPO**

Precise Competitor's Business Objective(s): **Invest in Technology**

Competitor's Strategic Capability (1-6, 6 being highest. Do scenario, if sc >= 3): **3**
[Build scenarios for organizations with sc >=3]

Your Organization's Business Objective(s): **To Be Technological Leader**

Does Dominant Environmental Force Affect Your Competitor's Objective(s)? (YES OR NO) **YES**

Does Dominant Environmental Force Affect Your Objective(s)? (YES OR NO) **YES**

Probability [HIGH/LOW] competitor will notice your moves: **HIGH**

COMMENTS: Assume that Mythical Air Bag Materials has a strategic capability rating of "5." The only question on the Strategic Capability form that Mythical Air Bag Materials received a "0" on was the following: "Is the organization making, or does it have the resources to make organization acquisitions?" And we will assume that Mythical Air Bag Materials can effectively respond to Competitor5's actions.

Fig. 6.15

Scenario and Simulation Analysis

SCENARIO 5 (continued)   **[SIMULATION FORM]**

(Take into account the environmental forces)

A. Competitor's Move(s):

     Check each of the following that apply to indicate what the competitor is doing or will likely do:

       lower/raise price ☐   specialize in a market ☐   be quality leader ☐   increase vertical integration ☐

       increase investment in technology ☒   achieve brand name ☐   add services ☐   collaborate ☐

       increase investment in marketing ☒

     Comments:

B. Your Response:

     Check each of the following that apply to indicate what your response is:

       ignore ☐   accommodate ☐   exit the market ☐   lower/raise price ☐   specialize in a market ☐

       be quality leader ☐   increase vertical integration ☐   increase investment in technology ☒

       achieve brand name ☐   add services ☐   collaborate ☐   increase investment in marketing ☐

     Comments:

C. Competitor's Response:

     Check each of the following that apply to indicate what your competitor's response is:

       ignore ☒   accommodate ☐   exit the market ☐   lower/raise price ☐   specialize in a market ☒

       be quality leader ☐   increase vertical integration ☐   increase investment in technology ☐

       achieve brand name ☐   add services ☐   collaborate ☐   increase investment in marketing ☒

     Comments:

D. Your Response:

     Check each of the following that apply to indicate what your response is:

       ignore ☐   accommodate ☐   exit the market ☐   lower/raise price ☐   specialize in a market ☐

       be quality leader ☐   increase vertical integration ☐   increase investment in technology ☒

       achieve brand name ☐   add services ☐   collaborate ☒   increase investment in marketing ☐

E. Your strategy to address scenario: **Increase tech investment; get SEC information to determine what competitor really does, if possible; look for collaborative opportunities.**

Fig. 6.16

Chapter 6

SCENARIO 6: Retrofitting Air Bags

Introduction: From Concept 6 above, we see that Competitor6 is an organization that will supply air bags to cars that didn't have them as original equipment. Assumptions and knowledge for this competitor are as follows:

- This organization will produce as much as possible in-house.

- This organization is trying to tap new financial resources.

- This organization wants to create another market segment within the air bag systems industry.

- This organization has relatively high strategic capability.

- This organization will notice our moves.

Despite the fact that this organization intends to be integrated, there may be an opportunity to sell our fabric to Competitor6, or one of Competitor6's suppliers. Using the results of our environmental forces analysis, our analysis of **Mythical Air Bag Materials'** business objectives in chapter 5, and the comments above, we now complete our scenario and simulation analysis for Competitor6.

Based on the above assumptions, we concluded that Competitor6 is trying to specialize in the air bag retrofit market. Of course, vertical integration is a consideration. Still, it is felt that the overriding objective here is to specialize in the retrofit market. Thus, the appropriate items supporting this competitor's objective are checked on the following three scenario-simulation pages. For example, on the SIMULATION INITIALIZATION FORM (figure 6.18), we indicate that this competitor is trying to specialize in a segment of the air bag systems industry. On the simulation form (figure 6.19), our check mark shows that we believe the competitor will increase its investment in marketing.

SCENARIO 6

COMPETITOR ACTIVITIES FORM

What is the competitor doing? Retrofitting air bags to cars not having them as original equipment

COMPETITOR BUSINESS OBJECTIVES FORM

"COMPETITOR'S" BUSINESS OBJECTIVES INDUSTRY: AIR BAG SYSTEMS COMPETITOR: Competitor6 (supplier)	INDICATE COMPETITOR'S BUSINESS OBJECTIVE(S) WITH A CHECK MARK.
To achieve low-price position	☐
To specialize in a market or market segment	☒
To sell the Top Quality Product/Service (Low product defect or low service error rate)	☐
To achieve vertical integration	☐
To be the technological leader	☐
To obtain brand identification	☐
To add service to product line	☐

STRATEGIC CAPABILITY FORM

COMPETITOR STRATEGIC CAPABILITY PARAMETER ESTIMATION INDUSTRY: AIR BAG SYSTEMS COMPETITOR: Competitor6	INDICATE "1" FOR YES, OR "0" FOR NO.
Is there enough demand for the product or service to support the existing competitors?	1
Is the organization making, or can it make an investment in technology?	1
Is the organization making, or does it have the resources to make organization acquisitions?	
Is the organization forming, or does it have the potential to form alliances or engage in some type of collaboration?	
Is the organization bringing in, or can the organization bring in high-powered personnel or management talent?	
Is the organization influencing, or can the organization influence market demand using its marketing strength or technology strength?	1
TOTAL (STRATEGIC CAPABILITY):	3

Fig. 6.17

Chapter 6

SIMULATION INITIALIZATION FORM

COMPETITOR: Competitor6
INDUSTRY: AIR BAG SYSTEMS

ASSUMPTIONS/KNOWLEDGE

Dominant Environmental Force(s) [Critical Success Factor(s)]: **Government**

Competitor's Move(s): **Retrofitting Air Bags to Cars Not Having Them**

Precise Competitor's Business Objective(s): **To Specialize in Retrofit Air Bag Market**

Competitor's Strategic Capability (1-6, 6 being highest. Do scenario, if sc >= 3): **3**
[Build scenarios for organizations with sc >=3]

Your Organization's Business Objective(s): **To Be Technological Leader in Air Bag Materials**

Does Dominant Environmental Force Affect Your Competitor's Objective(s)? (YES OR NO) **YES**

Does Dominant Environmental Force Affect Your Objective(s)? (YES OR NO) **YES**

Probability [HIGH/LOW] competitor will notice your moves: **HIGH**

COMMENTS: **Assume that Mythical Air Bag Materials has a strategic capability rating of "5." The only question on the Strategic Capability form that Mythical Air Bag Materials received a "0" on was the following:** "Is the organization making, or does it have the resources to make organization acquisitions?" And we will assume that Mythical Air Bag Materials can effectively respond to Competitor6's actions.

Fig. 6.18

Scenario and Simulation Analysis

SCENARIO 6 (continued)   **[SIMULATION FORM]**

(Take into account the environmental forces)

A. Competitor's Move(s):

Check each of the following that apply to indicate what the competitor is doing or will likely do:

lower/raise price ☐ specialize in a market ☒ be quality leader ☐ increase vertical integration ☐

increase investment in technology ☐ achieve brand name ☐ add services ☐ collaborate ☐

increase investment in marketing ☒

Comments: **We are not sure Competitor6 has the strategic capability to achieve its objective.**

B. Your Response:

Check each of the following that apply to indicate what your response is:

ignore ☐ accommodate ☐ exit the market ☐ lower/raise price ☐ specialize in a market ☐

be quality leader ☐ increase vertical integration ☐ increase investment in technology ☒

achieve brand name ☐ add services ☐ collaborate ☐ increase investment in marketing ☐

Comments: **Determine what fabric will be used.**

C. Competitor's Response:

Check each of the following that apply to indicate what your competitor's response is:

ignore ☒ accommodate ☐ exit the market ☐ lower/raise price ☐ specialize in a market ☐

be quality leader ☐ increase vertical integration ☐ increase investment in technology ☒

achieve brand name ☐ add services ☐ collaborate ☐ increase investment in marketing ☐

Comments:

D. Your Response:

Check each of the following that apply to indicate what your response is:

ignore ☐ accommodate ☐ exit the market ☐ lower/raise price ☐ specialize in a market ☐

be quality leader ☐ increase vertical integration ☐ increase investment in technology ☒

achieve brand name ☐ add services ☐ collaborate ☒ increase investment in marketing ☐

E. Your strategy to address scenario: **Increase investment in technology; increase investment in marketing; look for opportunities to make fabrics for the retrofit air bags.**

Fig. 6.19

Chapter 6

SCENARIO 7: Air Bag Modeling Technology

Introduction: From Concept 7 above, we see that Competitor7 is a large supplier of air bags and that Competitor7 is going to start using computer air bag modeling in its air bag research. Assumptions and knowledge for this competitor are as follows:

- This organization is willing to invest in technology.

- This organization has good financial resources.

- This organization is willing to pioneer new approaches.

- This organization has a high strategic capability.

- This organization will notice our moves.

If the computer models do not assume air bag fabric with our fabric's characteristics, this could be a threat, since it could lessen the buyers for our air bag fabric. If our fabric is included in the modeling, it could be an opportunity.

Using the results of our environmental forces analysis, our analysis of **Mythical Air Bag Materials'** business objectives in chapter 5, and the comments above, we now complete our scenario and simulation analysis for Competitor7.

Based on the assumptions above, it was felt that Competitor7 wanted to be a technology leader. So, appropriate items supporting this objective are checked on the simulation initialization and exercise pages (figures 6.21 and 6.22).

Scenario and Simulation Analysis

SCENARIO 7

COMPETITOR ACTIVITIES FORM

What is the competitor doing? Air Bag Systems supplier investing in computer air bag modeling technology

COMPETITOR BUSINESS OBJECTIVES FORM

"COMPETITOR'S" BUSINESS OBJECTIVES **INDUSTRY:** AIR BAG SYSTEMS **COMPETITOR:** Competitor7 (supplier)	INDICATE COMPETITOR'S BUSINESS OBJECTIVE(S) WITH A CHECK MARK.
To achieve low-price position	☐
To specialize in a market or market segment	☐
To sell the Top Quality Product/Service (Low product defect or low service error rate)	☐
To achieve vertical integration	☐
To be the technological leader	☒
To obtain brand identification	☐
To add service to product line	☐

STRATEGIC CAPABILITY FORM

COMPETITOR STRATEGIC CAPABILITY PARAMETER ESTIMATION **INDUSTRY:** AIR BAG SYSTEMS **COMPETITOR:** Competitor7	INDICATE "1" FOR YES, OR "0" FOR NO.
Is there enough demand for the product or service to support the existing competitors?	1
Is the organization making, or can it make an investment in technology?	1
Is the organization making, or does it have the resources to make organization acquisitions?	
Is the organization forming, or does it have the potential to form alliances or engage in some type of collaboration?	1
Is the organization bringing in, or can the organization bring in high-powered personnel or management talent?	1
Is the organization influencing, or can the organization influence market demand using its marketing strength or technology strength?	1
TOTAL (STRATEGIC CAPABILITY):	**5**

Fig. 6.20

155

Chapter 6

SIMULATION INITIALIZATION FORM

COMPETITOR: Competitor7
   INDUSTRY: AIR BAG SYSTEMS

ASSUMPTIONS/KNOWLEDGE

Dominant Environmental Force(s) [Critical Success Factor(s)]: **Government**

Competitor's Move(s): **Investing in Computer Air Bag Modeling Technology**

Precise Competitor's Business Objective(s): **To Be a Technological Leader in Air Bag Industry**

Competitor's Strategic Capability (1-6, 6 being highest. Do scenario, if sc >= 3): **5**
[Build scenarios for organizations with sc >=3]

Your Organization's Business Objective(s): **To Be a Technological Leader**

Does Dominant Environmental Force Affect Your Competitor's Objective(s)? (YES OR NO) **YES**

Does Dominant Environmental Force Affect Your Objective(s)? (YES OR NO) **YES**

Probability [HIGH/LOW] competitor will notice your moves: **HIGH**

COMMENTS: Assume that Mythical Air Bag Materials has a strategic capability rating of "5." The only question on the Strategic Capability form that Mythical Air Bag Materials received a "0" on was the following: "Is the organization making, or does it have the resources to make organization acquisitions?" And we will assume that Mythical Air Bag Materials can effectively respond to Competitor7's actions.

Fig. 6.21

Scenario and Simulation Analysis

SCENARIO 7 (continued)   **[SIMULATION FORM]**

(Take into account the environmental forces)

A. Competitor's Move(s):

Check each of the following that apply to indicate what the competitor is doing or will likely do:

lower/raise price ☐ specialize in a market ☐ be quality leader ☐ increase vertical integration ☐

increase investment in technology ☒ achieve brand name ☐ add services ☐ collaborate ☐

increase investment in marketing ☐

Comments:

B. Your Response:

Check each of the following that apply to indicate what your response is:

ignore ☐ accommodate ☐ exit the market ☐ lower/raise price ☐ specialize in a market ☐

be quality leader ☐ increase vertical integration ☐ increase investment in technology ☒

achieve brand name ☐ add services ☐ collaborate ☐ increase investment in marketing ☐

Comments: **Monitor; determine if our fabric is being modeled.**

C. Competitor's Response:

Check each of the following that apply to indicate what your competitor's response is:

ignore ☐ accommodate ☐ exit the market ☐ lower/raise price ☐ specialize in a market ☐

be quality leader ☐ increase vertical integration ☐ increase investment in technology ☒

achieve brand name ☐ add services ☐ collaborate ☐ increase investment in marketing ☐

Comments: **Competitor7 may monitor organizations like ours.**

D. Your Response:

Check each of the following that apply to indicate what your response is:

ignore ☐ accommodate ☐ exit the market ☐ lower/raise price ☐ specialize in a market ☐

be quality leader ☐ increase vertical integration ☐ increase investment in technology ☒

achieve brand name ☐ add services ☐ collaborate ☒ increase investment in marketing ☐

E. Your strategy to address scenario: **Look for opportunity to collaborate; continue to invest in technology.**

Fig. 6.22

157

Chapter 6

SCENARIO 8: Newer Type of Air Bags

Introduction: From Concept 8 above, we see that Competitor8, which is a large automobile manufacturer, expects to be using a new type of air bag in its automobiles. Assumptions and knowledge for this competitor are as follows:

- This organization wants to create the safest air bag possible.

- "Safest" is taken as a measure of quality.

- This organization wants to be first, with a new, safer air bag.

- This organization has a high strategic capability.

- This organization will notice our moves.

Our organization should try to contact this organization's suppliers to determine if we can supply them with our fabric. We need to determine what their requirements are. Using the results of our environmental forces analysis, our analysis of **Mythical Air Bag Materials'** business objectives in chapter 5, and the comments above, we now complete our scenario and simulation analysis for Competitor8.

Based on the assumptions above, it was concluded that Competitor8 wants to sell the highest quality automobiles. We assume that safety is a quality item. Therefore, items are checked on the following three scenario-simulation pages that support quality as the main competitive objective.

Scenario and Simulation Analysis

SCENARIO 8

COMPETITOR ACTIVITIES FORM

What is the competitor doing? Manufacturer is using newer type of air bag system in its automobiles

COMPETITOR BUSINESS OBJECTIVES FORM

"COMPETITOR'S" BUSINESS OBJECTIVES INDUSTRY: AIR BAG SYSTEMS COMPETITOR: Competitor8 (buyer)	INDICATE COMPETITOR'S BUSINESS OBJECTIVE(S) WITH A CHECK MARK.
To achieve low-price position	☐
To specialize in a market or market segment	☐
To sell the Top Quality Product/Service (Low product defect or low service error rate)	☒
To achieve vertical integration	☐
To be the technological leader	☐
To obtain brand identification	☐
To add service to product line	☐

STRATEGIC CAPABILITY FORM

COMPETITOR STRATEGIC CAPABILITY PARAMETER ESTIMATION INDUSTRY: AIR BAG SYSTEMS COMPETITOR: Competitor8	INDICATE "1" FOR YES, OR "0" FOR NO.
Is there enough demand for the product or service to support the existing competitors?	1
Is the organization making, or can it make an investment in technology?	1
Is the organization making, or does it have the resources to make organization acquisitions?	1
Is the organization forming, or does it have the potential to form alliances or engage in some type of collaboration?	1
Is the organization bringing in, or can the organization bring in high-powered personnel or management talent?	
Is the organization influencing, or can the organization influence market demand using its marketing strength or technology strength?	1
TOTAL (STRATEGIC CAPABILITY):	**5**

Fig. 6.23

Chapter 6

SIMULATION INITIALIZATION FORM

COMPETITOR: Competitor8
   INDUSTRY: AIR BAG SYSTEMS

ASSUMPTIONS/KNOWLEDGE

Dominant Environmental Force(s) [Critical Success Factor(s)]: **Government**

Competitor's Move(s): **Will Use Newer Type of Air Bag System**

Precise Competitor's Business Objective(s): **To Sell Safest Automobiles**

Competitor's Strategic Capability (1-6, 6 being highest. Do scenario, if sc >= 3): **5**
[Build scenarios for organizations with sc >=3]

Your Organization's Business Objective(s): **To Be Technological Leader in Air Bag Fabrics**

Does Dominant Environmental Force Affect Your Competitor's Objective(s)? (YES OR NO) **YES**

Does Dominant Environmental Force Affect Your Objective(s)? (YES OR NO) **YES**

Probability [HIGH/LOW] competitor will notice your moves: **HIGH**

COMMENTS: Assume that Mythical Air Bag Materials has a strategic capability rating of "5." The only question on the Strategic Capability form that Mythical Air Bag Materials received a "0" on was the following: "Is the organization making, or does it have the resources to make organization acquisitions?" And we will assume that Mythical Air Bag Materials can effectively respond to Competitor8's actions.

Fig. 6.24

Scenario and Simulation Analysis

(Take into account the environmental forces)

A. Competitor's Move(s):

Check each of the following that apply to indicate what the competitor is doing or will likely do:

lower/raise price ☐ specialize in a market ☐ be quality leader ☒ increase vertical integration ☐

increase investment in technology ☐ achieve brand name ☐ add services ☐ collaborate ☐

increase investment in marketing ☐

Comments: **We need to determine the supplier(s).**

B. Your Response:

Check each of the following that apply to indicate what your response is:

ignore ☐ accommodate ☐ exit the market ☐ lower/raise price ☐ specialize in a market ☐

be quality leader ☐ increase vertical integration ☐ increase investment in technology ☒

achieve brand name ☐ add services ☐ collaborate ☐ increase investment in marketing ☐

Comments: **Determine what materials the air bag systems will use.**

C. Competitor's Response:

Check each of the following that apply to indicate what your competitor's response is:

ignore ☐ accommodate ☐ exit the market ☐ lower/raise price ☐ specialize in a market ☐

be quality leader ☐ increase vertical integration ☐ increase investment in technology ☒

achieve brand name ☐ add services ☐ collaborate ☐ increase investment in marketing ☒

Comments: **Competitor8 may monitor us.**

D. Your Response:

Check each of the following that apply to indicate what your response is:

ignore ☐ accommodate ☐ exit the market ☐ lower/raise price ☐ specialize in a market ☐

be quality leader ☐ increase vertical integration ☐ increase investment in technology ☒

achieve brand name ☐ add services ☐ collaborate ☒ increase investment in marketing ☐

E. Your strategy to address scenario: **Monitor Competitor8; look into collaborating, if possible.**

Fig. 6.25

Chapter 6

SCENARIO 9: Low-Price Air Bags

Introduction: From Concept 9 above, we see that Competitor9 is a supplier of air bag systems and will produce a low-price air bag. Assumptions and knowledge for this competitor are as follows:

- This organization's air bags will be about one third the cost of most other air bags.

- This organization wants to be the low-price provider for air bag systems.

- This organization has relatively high strategic capability.

- This organization will notice our moves.

There is some concern within the industry that these air bags will not be as safe as the conventional air bags. We need to determine what's going on here. If this competitor can produce air bags at one third the cost of other air bags, this could be a threat to our organization. This could be a threat, because we would probably have to lower our fabric prices.

Using the results of our environmental forces analysis, our analysis of **Mythical Air Bag Materials'** business objectives in chapter 5, and the comments above, we now complete the scenario and simulation analysis for Competitor9.

Based on the above assumptions, we concluded that Competitor9 desires to create a low-price air bag. Thus, the appropriate items supporting this objective are checked on the following three scenario-simulation analysis pages.

Scenario and Simulation Analysis

SCENARIO 9

COMPETITOR ACTIVITIES FORM

What is the competitor doing? Introducing low cost air bag systems

COMPETITOR BUSINESS OBJECTIVES FORM

"COMPETITOR'S" BUSINESS OBJECTIVES INDUSTRY: AIR BAG SYSTEMS COMPETITOR: Competitor9 (supplier)	INDICATE COMPETITOR'S BUSINESS OBJECTIVE(S) WITH A CHECK MARK.
To achieve low-price position	☒
To specialize in a market or market segment	☐
To sell the Top Quality Product/Service (Low product defect or low service error rate)	☐
To achieve vertical integration	☐
To be the technological leader	☐
To obtain brand identification	☐
To add service to product line	☐

STRATEGIC CAPABILITY FORM

COMPETITOR STRATEGIC CAPABILITY PARAMETER ESTIMATION INDUSTRY: AIR BAG SYSTEMS COMPETITOR: Competitor9	INDICATE "1" FOR YES, OR "0" FOR NO.
Is there enough demand for the product or service to support the existing competitors?	1
Is the organization making, or can it make an investment in technology?	1
Is the organization making, or does it have the resources to make organization acquisitions?	
Is the organization forming, or does it have the potential to form alliances or engage in some type of collaboration?	
Is the organization bringing in, or can the organization bring in high-powered personnel or management talent?	
Is the organization influencing, or can the organization influence market demand using its marketing strength or technology strength?	1
TOTAL (STRATEGIC CAPABILITY):	**3**

Fig. 6.26

Chapter 6

SIMULATION INITIALIZATION FORM

COMPETITOR: Competitor9
   INDUSTRY: AIR BAG SYSTEMS

ASSUMPTIONS/KNOWLEDGE

Dominant Environmental Force(s) [Critical Success Factor(s)]: **Government**

Competitor's Move(s): **Introducing Low Cost Air Bag Systems**

Precise Competitor's Business Objective(s): **To Be a Low-Price Provider**

Competitor's Strategic Capability (1-6, 6 being highest. Do scenario, if sc >= 3): **3**
[Build scenarios for organizations with sc >=3]

Your Organization's Business Objective(s): **To Be Technological Leader in Air Bag Fabrics**

Does Dominant Environmental Force Affect Your Competitor's Objective(s)? (YES OR NO) **YES**

Does Dominant Environmental Force Affect Your Objective(s)? (YES OR NO) **YES**

Probability [HIGH/LOW] competitor will notice your moves: **HIGH**

COMMENTS: Assume that Mythical Air Bag Materials has a strategic capability rating of "5." The only question on the Strategic Capability form that Mythical Air Bag Materials received a "0" on was the following: "Is the organization making, or does it have the resources to make organization acquisitions?" And we will assume that Mythical Air Bag Materials can effectively respond to Competitor9's actions.

We would also like to know how Competitor9 is going to introduce a lower price air bag system.

Fig. 6.27

Scenario and Simulation Analysis

SCENARIO 9 (continued)   **[SIMULATION FORM]**

(Take into account the environmental forces)

A. Competitor's Move(s):

Check each of the following that apply to indicate what the competitor is doing or will likely do:

lower/raise price ☒ specialize in a market ☐ be quality leader ☐ increase vertical integration ☐

increase investment in technology ☐ achieve brand name ☐ add services ☐ collaborate ☐

increase investment in marketing ☐

Comments: **This organization wants to achieve a low-price position.**

B. Your Response:

Check each of the following that apply to indicate what your response is:

ignore ☐ accommodate ☐ exit the market ☐ lower/raise price ☐ specialize in a market ☐

be quality leader ☐ increase vertical integration ☐ increase investment in technology ☒

achieve brand name ☐ add services ☐ collaborate ☐ increase investment in marketing ☐

Comments:

C. Competitor's Response:

Check each of the following that apply to indicate what your competitor's response is:

ignore ☒ accommodate ☐ exit the market ☐ lower/raise price ☐ specialize in a market ☐

be quality leader ☐ increase vertical integration ☐ increase investment in technology ☐

achieve brand name ☒ add services ☐ collaborate ☐ increase investment in marketing ☒

Comments:

D. Your Response:

Check each of the following that apply to indicate what your response is:

ignore ☐ accommodate ☐ exit the market ☐ lower/raise price ☐ specialize in a market ☐

be quality leader ☐ increase vertical integration ☐ increase investment in technology ☒

achieve brand name ☐ add services ☐ collaborate ☐ increase investment in marketing ☐

E. Your strategy to address scenario: **Increase investment in technology. Determine how competitor can produce the low cost air bags; determine quality of material. See if collaboration is reasonable.**

Fig. 6.28

165

Chapter 6

SCENARIO 10: Purchasing an Air Bag Supplier

Introduction: From Concept 10 above, we see that Competitor10 is a producer of air bag systems and is purchasing another air bag systems competitor. Assumptions and knowledge for this competitor are as follows:

- This organization is interested in doing research and development.

- This organization is buying technology or talent.

- This organization might have the capability to produce air bag fabric.

- This organization has a relatively high strategic capability.

- This organization will notice our moves.

We need to determine if this competitor will now have the capability to produce its own fabric. Using the results of our environmental forces analysis, our analysis of **Mythical Air Bag Materials'** business objectives in chapter 5, and the comments above, we now complete the scenario and simulation analysis for Competitor10.

Based on the above assumptions, we felt that Competitor10's main objective is to be a leader in technology. On the following three pages, items supporting this objective are checked. This competitor may also be interested in becoming more integrated. For that reason, the box "increase vertical integration," is also checked in Level A of the simulation form (figure 6.31).

Scenario and Simulation Analysis

SCENARIO 10

COMPETITOR ACTIVITIES FORM

What is the competitor doing? Purchasing another air bag systems supplier

COMPETITOR BUSINESS OBJECTIVES FORM

"COMPETITOR'S" BUSINESS OBJECTIVES **INDUSTRY:** AIR BAG SYSTEMS **COMPETITOR:** Competitor10 (supplier)	INDICATE COMPETITOR'S BUSINESS OBJECTIVE(S) WITH A CHECK MARK.
To achieve low-price position	☐
To specialize in a market or market segment	☐
To sell the Top Quality Product/Service (Low product defect or low service error rate)	☐
To achieve vertical integration	☐
To be the technological leader	☒
To obtain brand identification	☐
To add service to product line	☐

STRATEGIC CAPABILITY FORM

COMPETITOR STRATEGIC CAPABILITY PARAMETER ESTIMATION **INDUSTRY:** AIR BAG SYSTEMS **COMPETITOR:** Competitor10	INDICATE "1" FOR YES, OR "0" FOR NO.
Is there enough demand for the product or service to support the existing competitors?	1
Is the organization making, or can it make an investment in technology?	1
Is the organization making, or does it have the resources to make organization acquisitions?	
Is the organization forming, or does it have the potential to form alliances or engage in some type of collaboration?	1
Is the organization bringing in, or can the organization bring in high-powered personnel or management talent?	1
Is the organization influencing, or can the organization influence market demand using its marketing strength or technology strength?	
TOTAL (STRATEGIC CAPABILITY):	**4**

Fig. 6.29

SCENARIO 10 (continued)

SIMULATION INITIALIZATION FORM

COMPETITOR: Competitor10
    INDUSTRY: AIR BAG SYSTEMS

ASSUMPTIONS/KNOWLEDGE

Dominant Environmental Force(s) [Critical Success Factor(s)]: **Government**

Competitor's Move(s): **Purchasing a Competitor**

Precise Competitor's Business Objective(s): **To Be a Technological Leader in Air Bag Systems**

Competitor's Strategic Capability (1-6, 6 being highest. Do scenario, if sc >= 3): **4**
[Build scenarios for organizations with sc >=3]

Your Organization's Business Objective(s): **To Be Technological Leader in Air Bag Fabrics**

Does Dominant Environmental Force Affect Your Competitor's Objective(s)? (YES OR NO) **YES**

Does Dominant Environmental Force Affect Your Objective(s)? (YES OR NO) **YES**

Probability [HIGH/LOW] competitor will notice your moves: **HIGH**

COMMENTS: Assume that Mythical Air Bag Materials has a strategic capability rating of "5." The only question on the Strategic Capability form that Mythical Air Bag Materials received a "0" on was the following: "Is the organization making, or does it have the resources to make organization acquisitions?" And we will assume that Mythical Air Bag Materials can effectively respond to Competitor10's actions.

Fig. 6.30

Scenario and Simulation Analysis

SCENARIO 10 (continued)   **[SIMULATION FORM]**

(Take into account the environmental forces)

A. Competitor's Move(s):

Check each of the following that apply to indicate what the competitor is doing or will likely do:

lower/raise price ☐   specialize in a market ☐   be quality leader ☐   increase vertical integration ☒

increase investment in technology ☒   achieve brand name ☐   add services ☐   collaborate ☐

increase investment in marketing ☐

Comments:

B. Your Response:

Check each of the following that apply to indicate what your response is:

ignore ☐   accommodate ☐   exit the market ☐   lower/raise price ☐   specialize in a market ☐

be quality leader ☐   increase vertical integration ☐   increase investment in technology ☒

achieve brand name ☐   add services ☐   collaborate ☐   increase investment in marketing ☐

Comments:

C. Competitor's Response:

Check each of the following that apply to indicate what your competitor's response is:

ignore ☐   accommodate ☐   exit the market ☐   lower/raise price ☐   specialize in a market ☐

be quality leader ☐   increase vertical integration ☐   increase investment in technology ☐

achieve brand name ☐   add services ☐   collaborate ☐   increase investment in marketing ☒

Comments: **Competitor10 will probably monitor us.**

D. Your Response:

Check each of the following that apply to indicate what your response is:

ignore ☐   accommodate ☐   exit the market ☐   lower/raise price ☐   specialize in a market ☐

be quality leader ☐   increase vertical integration ☐   increase investment in technology ☒

achieve brand name ☐   add services ☐   collaborate ☐   increase investment in marketing ☐

E. Your strategy to address scenario: **Invest in technology; monitor Competitor10 to see if they will produce air bag fabrics.**

Fig. 6.31

Chapter 6

SCENARIO 11: First to Offer Side Air Bags

Introduction: From Concept 11 above, we see that Competitor11 is an automobile manufacturer that wants to be the first manufacturer to provide side air bag systems. Assumptions and knowledge for this competitor are as follows:

- This organization is very interested in new technology.

- This organization's main air bag systems supplier makes its own air bag fabric.

- This organization has a relatively high strategic capability.

- This organization will notice our moves.

We need to see if we can become the fabric supplier for this air bag systems supplier. Using the results of our environmental forces analysis, our analysis of **Mythical Air Bag Materials'** business objectives in chapter 5, and the comments above, we now complete our scenario and simulation analysis for Competitor11.

Based on the above assumptions, Competitor11 is interested in selling automobiles with the latest air bag technology. On the next three pages, appropriate items supporting this competitor objective are checked for the scenario-simulation analysis.

Scenario and Simulation Analysis

SCENARIO 11

COMPETITOR ACTIVITIES FORM

What is the competitor doing? Trying to be first to offer side air bag systems

COMPETITOR BUSINESS OBJECTIVES FORM

"COMPETITOR'S" BUSINESS OBJECTIVES INDUSTRY: AIR BAG SYSTEMS COMPETITOR: Competitor11 (buyer)	INDICATE COMPETITOR'S BUSINESS OBJECTIVE(S) WITH A CHECK MARK.
To achieve low-price position	☐
To specialize in a market or market segment	☐
To sell the Top Quality Product/Service (Low product defect or low service error rate)	☐
To achieve vertical integration	☐
To be the technological leader	☒
To obtain brand identification	☐
To add service to product line	☐

STRATEGIC CAPABILITY FORM

COMPETITOR STRATEGIC CAPABILITY PARAMETER ESTIMATION INDUSTRY: AIR BAG SYSTEMS COMPETITOR: Competitor11	INDICATE "1" FOR YES, OR "0" FOR NO.
Is there enough demand for the product or service to support the existing competitors?	1
Is the organization making, or can it make an investment in technology?	1
Is the organization making, or does it have the resources to make organization acquisitions?	
Is the organization forming, or does it have the potential to form alliances or engage in some type of collaboration?	
Is the organization bringing in, or can the organization bring in high-powered personnel or management talent?	1
Is the organization influencing, or can the organization influence market demand using its marketing strength or technology strength?	1
TOTAL (STRATEGIC CAPABILITY):	4

Fig. 6.32

171

Chapter 6

SIMULATION INITIALIZATION FORM

COMPETITOR: Competitor11
    INDUSTRY: AIR BAG SYSTEMS

ASSUMPTIONS/KNOWLEDGE

Dominant Environmental Force(s) [Critical Success Factor(s)]: **Government**

Competitor's Move(s): **Making Technology Investment**

Precise Competitor's Business Objective(s): **Become a Technological Leader (Side Air Bag Systems)**

Competitor's Strategic Capability (1-6, 6 being highest. Do scenario, if sc >= 3): **4**
[Build scenarios for organizations with sc >=3]

Your Organization's Business Objective(s): **To Be Technological Leader in Air Bag Fabrics**

Does Dominant Environmental Force Affect Your Competitor's Objective(s)? (YES OR NO) **YES**

Does Dominant Environmental Force Affect Your Objective(s)? (YES OR NO) **YES**

Probability [HIGH/LOW] competitor will notice your moves: **HIGH**

COMMENTS: Assume that Mythical Air Bag Materials has a strategic capability rating of "5." The only question on the Strategic Capability form that Mythical Air Bag Materials received a "0" on was the following: "Is the organization making, or does it have the resources to make organization acquisitions?" And we will assume that Mythical Air Bag Materials can effectively respond to Competitor11's actions.

Fig. 6.33

Scenario and Simulation Analysis

SCENARIO 11 (continued)   **[SIMULATION FORM]**

(Take into account the environmental forces)

A. Competitor's Move(s):

Check each of the following that apply to indicate what the competitor is doing or will likely do:

lower/raise price ☐ specialize in a market ☐ be quality leader ☐ increase vertical integration ☐

increase investment in technology ☒ achieve brand name ☐ add services ☐ collaborate ☐

increase investment in marketing ☐

Comments:

B. Your Response:

Check each of the following that apply to indicate what your response is:

ignore ☐ accommodate ☐ exit the market ☐ lower/raise price ☐ specialize in a market ☐

be quality leader ☐ increase vertical integration ☐ increase investment in technology ☒

achieve brand name ☐ add services ☐ collaborate ☐ increase investment in marketing ☐

Comments:

C. Competitor's Response:

Check each of the following that apply to indicate what your competitor's response is:

ignore ☐ accommodate ☐ exit the market ☐ lower/raise price ☐ specialize in a market ☐

be quality leader ☐ increase vertical integration ☐ increase investment in technology ☒

achieve brand name ☐ add services ☐ collaborate ☐ increase investment in marketing ☐

Comments:

D. Your Response:

Check each of the following that apply to indicate what your response is:

ignore ☐ accommodate ☐ exit the market ☐ lower/raise price ☐ specialize in a market ☐

be quality leader ☐ increase vertical integration ☐ increase investment in technology ☒

achieve brand name ☐ add services ☐ collaborate ☒ increase investment in marketing ☐

E. Your strategy to address scenario: **Invest in technology; look for collaborative opportunities.**

Fig. 6.34

173

Chapter 6

SCENARIO 12: New Personnel

Introduction: From Concept 12 above, we see that Competitor12 is a supplier of air bag systems, and the organization is bringing in new personnel. Assumptions and knowledge for this competitor are as follows:

- This organization subcontracts out its air bag fabric production.

- This organization is interested in doing more research and development.

- This organization's new personnel are highly educated with research experience.

- This organization has a relatively high strategic capability.

- This organization will notice our moves.

We will look for collaborative opportunities, here. We believe that this competitor is trying to increase its air bag production. Using the results of our environmental forces analysis, our analysis of **Mythical Air Bag Materials'** business objectives in chapter 5, and the comments above, we now complete our scenario and simulation analysis for Competitor12.

Based on the assumptions above, and on the fact that Competitor12 is bringing in new people with research experience, it was felt that this competitor's main objective is probably to invest more in research and development. We will view this as an investment in technology. Therefore, appropriate items supporting this objective are checked on the next three scenario-simulation pages.

SCENARIO 12

COMPETITOR ACTIVITIES FORM

What is the competitor doing? Air bag systems supplier bringing in new personnel

COMPETITOR BUSINESS OBJECTIVES FORM

"COMPETITOR'S" BUSINESS OBJECTIVES **INDUSTRY:** AIR BAG SYSTEMS **COMPETITOR:** Competitor12 (supplier)	**INDICATE COMPETITOR'S BUSINESS OBJECTIVE(S) WITH A CHECK MARK.**
To achieve low-price position	☐
To specialize in a market or market segment	☐
To sell the Top Quality Product/Service (Low product defect or low service error rate)	☐
To achieve vertical integration	☐
To be the technological leader	☒
To obtain brand identification	☐
To add service to product line	☐

STRATEGIC CAPABILITY FORM

COMPETITOR **STRATEGIC CAPABILITY PARAMETER ESTIMATION** **INDUSTRY:** AIR BAG SYSTEMS **COMPETITOR:** Competitor12	**INDICATE "1" FOR YES, OR "0" FOR NO.**
Is there enough demand for the product or service to support the existing competitors?	1
Is the organization making, or can it make an investment in technology?	
Is the organization making, or does it have the resources to make organization acquisitions?	
Is the organization forming, or does it have the potential to form alliances or engage in some type of collaboration?	1
Is the organization bringing in, or can the organization bring in high-powered personnel or management talent?	1
Is the organization influencing, or can the organization influence market demand using its marketing strength or technology strength?	
TOTAL (STRATEGIC CAPABILITY):	3

Fig. 6.35

SCENARIO 12 (continued)

SIMULATION INITIALIZATION FORM

COMPETITOR: Competitor12
   INDUSTRY: AIR BAG SYSTEMS

ASSUMPTIONS/KNOWLEDGE

Dominant Environmental Force(s) [Critical Success Factor(s)]: **Government**

Competitor's Move(s): **Bringing in New Personnel**

Precise Competitor's Business Objective(s): **To Be a Technological Leader in Non-Fabric Components**

Competitor's Strategic Capability (1-6, 6 being highest. Do scenario, if sc >= 3): **3**
[Build scenarios for organizations with sc >=3]

Your Organization's Business Objective(s): **To Be Technological Leader in Air Bag Fabrics**

Does Dominant Environmental Force Affect Your Competitor's Objective(s)? (YES OR NO) **YES**

Does Dominant Environmental Force Affect Your Objective(s)? (YES OR NO) **YES**

Probability [HIGH/LOW] competitor will notice your moves: **HIGH**

COMMENTS: Assume that Mythical Air Bag Materials has a strategic capability rating of "5." The only question on the Strategic Capability form that Mythical Air Bag Materials received a "0" on was the following: "Is the organization making, or does it have the resources to make organization acquisitions?" And we will assume that Mythical Air Bag Materials can effectively respond to Competitor12's actions.

Fig. 6.36

Scenario and Simulation Analysis

SCENARIO 12 (continued)   **[SIMULATION FORM]**

(Take into account the environmental forces):

A. Competitor's Move(s):

Check each of the following that apply to indicate what the competitor is doing or will likely do:

lower/raise price ☐ specialize in a market ☐ be quality leader ☐ increase vertical integration ☐

increase investment in technology ☒ achieve brand name ☐ add services ☐ collaborate ☐

increase investment in marketing ☐

Comments:

B. Your Response:

Check each of the following that apply to indicate what your response is:

ignore ☐ accommodate ☐ exit the market ☐ lower/raise price ☐ specialize in a market ☐

be quality leader ☐ increase vertical integration ☐ increase investment in technology ☒

achieve brand name ☐ add services ☐ collaborate ☐ increase investment in marketing ☐

Comments: Determine if the competitor may produce air bag fabric.

C. Competitor's Response:

Check each of the following that apply to indicate what your competitor's response is:

ignore ☐ accommodate ☐ exit the market ☐ lower/raise price ☐ specialize in a market ☐

be quality leader ☐ increase vertical integration ☒ increase investment in technology ☒

achieve brand name ☐ add services ☐ collaborate ☐ increase investment in marketing ☐

Comments:

D. Your Response:

Check each of the following that apply to indicate what your response is:

ignore ☐ accommodate ☐ exit the market ☐ lower/raise price ☐ specialize in a market ☐

be quality leader ☐ increase vertical integration ☐ increase investment in technology ☒

achieve brand name ☐ add services ☐ collaborate ☐ increase investment in marketing ☐

E. Your strategy to address scenario: **Invest in technology; continue to monitor the competitor.**

Fig. 6.37

SCENARIO 13: Reducing Air Bag Size

Introduction: From Concept 13 above, we see that Competitor13 is a supplier of air bags and will start producing smaller air bags. Assumptions and knowledge for this competitor are as follows:

- This organization invests heavily in technology.

- This organization outsources its fabric production.

- This organization has a relatively high strategic capability.

- This organization will notice our moves.

We need to try to get the contract to produce the fabric for this competitor. We believe our fabric will allow a reduced-size air bag. Using the results of our environmental forces analysis, our analysis of **Mythical Air Bag Materials'** business objectives in chapter 5, and the comments above, we now complete our scenario and simulation analysis for Competitor13.

Based on the assumptions above, it was concluded that Competitor13 desires to be a leader in technology in the air bag systems industry. Therefore, items are checked on the following scenario-simulation pages which support this competitor's objective.

Scenario and Simulation Analysis

SCENARIO 13

COMPETITOR ACTIVITIES FORM

What is the competitor doing? Air bag systems supplier reducing the size of air bags

COMPETITOR BUSINESS OBJECTIVES FORM

"COMPETITOR'S" BUSINESS OBJECTIVES INDUSTRY: AIR BAG SYSTEMS COMPETITOR: Competitor13 (supplier)	INDICATE COMPETITOR'S BUSINESS OBJECTIVE(S) WITH A CHECK MARK.
To achieve low-price position	☐
To specialize in a market or market segment	☐
To sell the Top Quality Product/Service (Low product defect or low service error rate)	☐
To achieve vertical integration	☐
To be the technological leader	☒
To obtain brand identification	☐
To add service to product line	☐

STRATEGIC CAPABILITY FORM

COMPETITOR STRATEGIC CAPABILITY PARAMETER ESTIMATION INDUSTRY: AIR BAG SYSTEMS COMPETITOR: Competitor13	INDICATE "1" FOR YES, OR "0" FOR NO.
Is there enough demand for the product or service to support the existing competitors?	1
Is the organization making, or can it make an investment in technology?	1
Is the organization making, or does it have the resources to make organization acquisitions?	
Is the organization forming, or does it have the potential to form alliances or engage in some type of collaboration?	
Is the organization bringing in, or can the organization bring in high-powered personnel or management talent?	
Is the organization influencing, or can the organization influence market demand using its marketing strength or technology strength?	1
TOTAL (STRATEGIC CAPABILITY):	3

Fig. 6.38

Chapter 6

SIMULATION INITIALIZATION FORM

COMPETITOR: Competitor13
   INDUSTRY: AIR BAG SYSTEMS

ASSUMPTIONS/KNOWLEDGE

Dominant Environmental Force(s) [Critical Success Factor(s)]: **Government**

Competitor's Move(s): **Reducing the Size of Air Bags**

Precise Competitor's Business Objective(s): **To Be a Technological Leader (Reduced-Size Air Bags)**

Competitor's Strategic Capability (1-6, 6 being highest. Do scenario, if sc >= 3): **3**
[Build scenarios for organizations with sc >=3]

Your Organization's Business Objective(s): **To Be Technological Leader in Air Bag Fabrics**

Does Dominant Environmental Force Affect Your Competitor's Objective(s)? (YES OR NO) **YES**

Does Dominant Environmental Force Affect Your Objective(s)? (YES OR NO) **YES**

Probability [HIGH/LOW] competitor will notice your moves: **HIGH**

COMMENTS: Assume that Mythical Air Bag Materials has a strategic capability rating of "5." The only question on the Strategic Capability form that Mythical Air Bag Materials received a "0" on was the following: "Is the organization making, or does it have the resources to make organization acquisitions?" And we will assume that Mythical Air Bag Materials can effectively respond to Competitor13's actions.

Fig. 6.39

Scenario and Simulation Analysis

SCENARIO 13 (continued)   **[SIMULATION FORM]**

(Take into account the environmental forces)

A. Competitor's Move(s):

Check each of the following that apply to indicate what the competitor is doing or will likely do:

lower/raise price ☐ specialize in a market ☐ be quality leader ☐ increase vertical integration ☐

increase investment in technology ☒ achieve brand name ☐ add services ☐ collaborate ☐

increase investment in marketing ☐

Comments:

B. Your Response:

Check each of the following that apply to indicate what your response is:

ignore ☐ accommodate ☐ exit the market ☐ lower/raise price ☐ specialize in a market ☐

be quality leader ☐ increase vertical integration ☐ increase investment in technology ☒

achieve brand name ☐ add services ☐ collaborate ☐ increase investment in marketing ☐

Comments: **Determine if our fabric is compatible with the reduced-size air bags.**

C. Competitor's Response:

Check each of the following that apply to indicate what your competitor's response is:

ignore ☐ accommodate ☐ exit the market ☐ lower/raise price ☐ specialize in a market ☐

be quality leader ☐ increase vertical integration ☐ increase investment in technology ☒

achieve brand name ☐ add services ☐ collaborate ☐ increase investment in marketing ☐

Comments: **Competitor13 may be open to collaboration with us.**

D. Your Response:

Check each of the following that apply to indicate what your response is:

ignore ☐ accommodate ☐ exit the market ☐ lower/raise price ☐ specialize in a market ☐

be quality leader ☐ increase vertical integration ☐ increase investment in technology ☒

achieve brand name ☐ add services ☐ collaborate ☐ increase investment in marketing ☐

E. Your strategy to address scenario: **Invest in technology; look for collaborative opportunities.**

Fig. 6.40

Chapter 6

SCENARIO 14: Rear Seat Air Bags

Introduction: From Concept 14 above, we see that Competitor14 is a large automobile manufacturer and wants to be the first to offer rear seat air bags. Assumptions and knowledge for this competitor are as follows:

- This organization wants to sell the safest automobiles.

- This organization is interested in any other components maker that might help Competitor14 sell the safest automobiles.

- This organization has a relatively high strategic capability.

- This organization will notice our moves.

We need to see if collaborative opportunities are available. Using the results of our environmental forces analysis, our analysis of **Mythical Air Bag Materials'** business objectives in chapter 5, and the comments above, we now complete our scenario and simulation analysis for Competitor14.

Based on the assumptions above, we concluded that Competitor14 desires to sell the highest quality automobiles which, the competitor believes, should include rear seat air bags. On the following three scenario-simulation pages, items supporting this objective are checked.

Scenario and Simulation Analysis

SCENARIO 14

COMPETITOR ACTIVITIES FORM

What is the competitor doing? Preparing to be the first automobile manufacturer to offer rear seat air bag systems

COMPETITOR BUSINESS OBJECTIVES FORM

"COMPETITOR'S" BUSINESS OBJECTIVES INDUSTRY: AIR BAG SYSTEMS COMPETITOR: Competitor14 (buyer)	INDICATE COMPETITOR'S BUSINESS OBJECTIVE(S) WITH A CHECK MARK.
To achieve low-price position	☐
To specialize in a market or market segment	☐
To sell the Top Quality Product/Service (Low product defect or low service error rate)	☒
To achieve vertical integration	☐
To be the technological leader	☐
To obtain brand identification	☐
To add service to product line	☐

STRATEGIC CAPABILITY FORM

COMPETITOR STRATEGIC CAPABILITY PARAMETER ESTIMATION INDUSTRY: AIR BAG SYSTEMS COMPETITOR: Competitor14	INDICATE "1" FOR YES, OR "0" FOR NO.
Is there enough demand for the product or service to support the existing competitors?	1
Is the organization making, or can it make an investment in technology?	1
Is the organization making, or does it have the resources to make organization acquisitions?	
Is the organization forming, or does it have the potential to form alliances or engage in some type of collaboration?	
Is the organization bringing in, or can the organization bring in high-powered personnel or management talent?	
Is the organization influencing, or can the organization influence market demand using its marketing strength or technology strength?	1
TOTAL (STRATEGIC CAPABILITY):	3

Fig. 6.41

SCENARIO 14 (continued)

SIMULATION INITIALIZATION FORM

COMPETITOR: Competitor14
   INDUSTRY: AIR BAG SYSTEMS

ASSUMPTIONS/KNOWLEDGE

Dominant Environmental Force(s) [Critical Success Factor(s)]: **Government**

Competitor's Move(s): **Taking Action to Be the First to Offer a Rear Seat Air Bag**

Precise Competitor's Business Objective(s): **Sell Safest Automobiles**

Competitor's Strategic Capability (1-6, 6 being highest. Do scenario, if sc >= 3): **3**
[Build scenarios for organizations with sc >=3]

Your Organization's Business Objective(s): **To Be Technological Leader in Air Bag Fabrics**

Does Dominant Environmental Force Affect Your Competitor's Objective(s)? (YES OR NO) **YES**

Does Dominant Environmental Force Affect Your Objective(s)? (YES OR NO) **YES**

Probability [HIGH/LOW] competitor will notice your moves: **HIGH**

COMMENTS: Assume that Mythical Air Bag Materials has a strategic capability rating of "5." The only question on the Strategic Capability form that Mythical Air Bag Materials received a "0" on was the following: "Is the organization making, or does it have the resources to make organization acquisitions?" And we will assume that Mythical Air Bag Materials can effectively respond to Competitor14's actions.

Fig. 6.42

Scenario and Simulation Analysis

SCENARIO 14 (continued)   **[SIMULATION FORM]**

(Take into account the environmental forces)

A. Competitor's Move(s):

   Check each of the following that apply to indicate what the competitor is doing or will likely do:

   lower/raise price ☐   specialize in a market ☐   be quality leader ☒   increase vertical integration ☐

   increase investment in technology ☐   achieve brand name ☐   add services ☐   collaborate ☐

   increase investment in marketing ☐

   Comments:

B. Your Response:

   Check each of the following that apply to indicate what your response is:

   ignore ☐   accommodate ☐   exit the market ☐   lower/raise price ☐   specialize in a market ☐

   be quality leader ☐   increase vertical integration ☐   increase investment in technology ☒

   achieve brand name ☐   add services ☐   collaborate ☐   increase investment in marketing ☐

   Comments:

C. Competitor's Response:

   Check each of the following that apply to indicate what your competitor's response is:

   ignore ☐   accommodate ☒   exit the market ☐   lower/raise price ☐   specialize in a market ☐

   be quality leader ☐   increase vertical integration ☐   increase investment in technology ☐

   achieve brand name ☐   add services ☐   collaborate ☐   increase investment in marketing ☐

   Comments:

D. Your Response:

   Check each of the following that apply to indicate what your response is:

   ignore ☐   accommodate ☐   exit the market ☐   lower/raise price ☐   specialize in a market ☐

   be quality leader ☐   increase vertical integration ☐   increase investment in technology ☒

   achieve brand name ☐   add services ☐   collaborate ☒   increase investment in marketing ☐

E. Your strategy to address scenario: **Invest in technology; determine what kind of fabric is used in the competitor's air bags. This could be a threat if the fabric is quite different from our fabric.**

Fig. 6.43

185

Chapter 6

SCENARIO 15: Contract to Supply Mini Air Bags

Introduction: From Concept 15 above, we see that Competitor15 has received a large contract to supply mini air bags. Assumptions and knowledge for this competitor are as follows:

- This organization was able to keep its bid for the contract a secret.

- This organization has resources to invest in technology.

- This organization has a relatively high strategic capability.

- This organization will notice our moves.

We need to determine if we can create some opportunities for our organization. Using the results of our environmental forces analysis, our analysis of **Mythical Air Bag Materials'** business objectives in chapter 5, and the comments above, we now complete our scenario and simulation analysis for Competitor15.

Based on the above assumptions, we concluded that Competitor15's main objective was to be a leader in technology. Mini air bags serve the same purpose as normal size (larger) air bags, but mini air bags can fit into smaller places which means that the air bags may contain new technology. Since it was felt that this competitor wanted to be a leader in technology, appropriate items supporting this objective are checked on the following three scenario-simulation pages.

Scenario and Simulation Analysis

SCENARIO 15

COMPETITOR ACTIVITIES FORM

What is the competitor doing? Obtained major contract to supply mini air bags to an automobile manufacturer

COMPETITOR BUSINESS OBJECTIVES FORM

"COMPETITOR'S" BUSINESS OBJECTIVES INDUSTRY: AIR BAG SYSTEMS COMPETITOR: Competitor15 (supplier)	INDICATE COMPETITOR'S BUSINESS OBJECTIVE(S) WITH A CHECK MARK.
To achieve low-price position	☐
To specialize in a market or market segment	☐
To sell the Top Quality Product/Service (Low product defect or low service error rate)	☐
To achieve vertical integration	☐
To be the technological leader	☒
To obtain brand identification	☐
To add service to product line	☐

STRATEGIC CAPABILITY FORM

COMPETITOR STRATEGIC CAPABILITY PARAMETER ESTIMATION INDUSTRY: AIR BAG SYSTEMS COMPETITOR: Competitor15	INDICATE "1" FOR YES, OR "0" FOR NO.
Is there enough demand for the product or service to support the existing competitors?	1
Is the organization making, or can it make an investment in technology?	1
Is the organization making, or does it have the resources to make organization acquisitions?	
Is the organization forming, or does it have the potential to form alliances or engage in some type of collaboration?	1
Is the organization bringing in, or can the organization bring in high-powered personnel or management talent?	
Is the organization influencing, or can the organization influence market demand using its marketing strength or technology strength?	
TOTAL (STRATEGIC CAPABILITY):	**3**

Fig. 6.44

187

SCENARIO 15 (continued)

SIMULATION INITIALIZATION FORM

COMPETITOR: Competitor15
    INDUSTRY: AIR BAG SYSTEMS

ASSUMPTIONS/KNOWLEDGE

Dominant Environmental Force(s) [Critical Success Factor(s)]: **Government**

Competitor's Move(s): **Obtained Major Contract to Supply Mini Air Bag System to Top Auto Maker**

Precise Competitor's Business Objective(s): **Technological Leader in Mini Air Bags**

Competitor's Strategic Capability (1-6, 6 being highest. Do scenario, if sc >= 3): **3**
[Build scenarios for organizations with sc >=3]

Your Organization's Business Objective(s): **To Be Technological Leader in Air Bag Fabrics**

Does Dominant Environmental Force Affect Your Competitor's Objective(s)? (YES OR NO) **YES**

Does Dominant Environmental Force Affect Your Objective(s)? (YES OR NO) **YES**

Probability [HIGH/LOW] competitor will notice your moves: **HIGH**

COMMENTS: Assume that Mythical Air Bag Materials has a strategic capability rating of "5." The only question on the Strategic Capability form that Mythical Air Bag Materials received a "0" on was the following: "Is the organization making, or does it have the resources to make organization acquisitions?" And we will assume that Mythical Air Bag Materials can effectively respond to Competitor15's actions.

Fig. 6.45

Scenario and Simulation Analysis

SCENARIO 15 (continued)   **[SIMULATION FORM]**

(Take into account the environmental forces)

A. Competitor's Move(s):

Check each of the following that apply to indicate what the competitor is doing or will likely do:

lower/raise price ☐   specialize in a market ☐   be quality leader ☐   increase vertical integration ☐

increase investment in technology ☒   achieve brand name ☐   add services ☐   collaborate ☐

increase investment in marketing ☐

Comments: **Competitor15 will be offering mini air bag systems.**

B. Your Response:

Check each of the following that apply to indicate what your response is:

ignore ☐   accommodate ☐   exit the market ☐   lower/raise price ☐   specialize in a market ☐

be quality leader ☐   increase vertical integration ☐   increase investment in technology ☒

achieve brand name ☐   add services ☐   collaborate ☐   increase investment in marketing ☐

Comments: **Determine if our fabric is compatible with mini systems.**

C. Competitor's Response:

Check each of the following that apply to indicate what your competitor's response is:

ignore ☒   accommodate ☐   exit the market ☐   lower/raise price ☐   specialize in a market ☐

be quality leader ☐   increase vertical integration ☐   increase investment in technology ☒

achieve brand name ☒   add services ☐   collaborate ☐   increase investment in marketing ☐

Comments:

D. Your Response:

Check each of the following that apply to indicate what your response is:

ignore ☐   accommodate ☐   exit the market ☐   lower/raise price ☐   specialize in a market ☐

be quality leader ☐   increase vertical integration ☐   increase investment in technology ☐

achieve brand name ☐   add services ☐   collaborate ☒   increase investment in marketing ☒

E. Your strategy to address scenario: **Invest in technology; look for collaborative opportunities.**

Fig. 6.46

Chapter 6

SCENARIO 16: Inventor Introducing Lower Price Air Bags

Introduction: From Concept 16 above, we see that Competitor16 is an inventor who plans to develop safer, lower-priced air bags. Assumptions and knowledge for this competitor are as follows:

- This inventor has a competitive product and is a potential entrant to the air bag industry.

- This potential competitor has a relatively high strategic capability.

- If this inventor starts an organization, the organization will notice our moves.

Our organization needs to determine if there is new fabric technology that our organization is not aware of which is inexpensive enough to help this potential competitor produce a low-price air bag. Using the results of our environmental forces analysis, our analysis of **Mythical Air Bag Materials'** business objectives in chapter 5, and the comments above, we now complete our scenario and simulation analysis for Competitor16.

Based on the above assumptions, we decided that Competitor16's major objective is to produce a low-price air bag. Therefore, on the following three scenario-simulation pages, items supporting this competitor's objective are checked. Since we believe that the competitor will have to increase investment in technology, we indicate this on the simulation form (figure 6.49).

SCENARIO 16

COMPETITOR ACTIVITIES FORM

What is the competitor doing? Inventor plans to develop and market safer, lower-priced air bag systems

COMPETITOR BUSINESS OBJECTIVES FORM

"COMPETITOR'S" BUSINESS OBJECTIVES INDUSTRY: AIR BAG SYSTEMS COMPETITOR: Competitor16 (potential entrant)	INDICATE COMPETITOR'S BUSINESS OBJECTIVE(S) WITH A CHECK MARK.
To achieve low-price position	☒
To specialize in a market or market segment	☐
To sell the Top Quality Product/Service (Low product defect or low service error rate)	☐
To achieve vertical integration	☐
To be the technological leader	☐
To obtain brand identification	☐
To add service to product line	☐

STRATEGIC CAPABILITY FORM

COMPETITOR STRATEGIC CAPABILITY PARAMETER ESTIMATION INDUSTRY: AIR BAG SYSTEMS COMPETITOR: Competitor16	INDICATE "1" FOR YES, OR "0" FOR NO.
Is there enough demand for the product or service to support the existing competitors?	1
Is the organization making, or can it make an investment in technology?	1
Is the organization making, or does it have the resources to make organization acquisitions?	
Is the organization forming, or does it have the potential to form alliances or engage in some type of collaboration?	
Is the organization bringing in, or can the organization bring in high-powered personnel or management talent?	1
Is the organization influencing, or can the organization influence market demand using its marketing strength or technology strength?	
TOTAL (STRATEGIC CAPABILITY):	**3**

Fig. 6.47

Chapter 6

SIMULATION INITIALIZATION FORM

COMPETITOR: Competitor16
   INDUSTRY: AIR BAG SYSTEMS

ASSUMPTIONS/KNOWLEDGE

Dominant Environmental Force(s) [Critical Success Factor(s)]: **Government**

Competitor's Move(s): **Plans to Develop and Market Safer, Lower-Priced Air Bag Systems**

Precise Competitor's Business Objective(s): **To Achieve a Low-Price Position in Air Bag Market**

Competitor's Strategic Capability (1-6, 6 being highest. Do scenario, if sc >= 3): **3**
[Build scenarios for organizations with sc >=3]

Your Organization's Business Objective(s): **To Be Technological Leader in Air Bag Fabrics**

Does Dominant Environmental Force Affect Your Competitor's Objective(s)? (YES OR NO) **YES**

Does Dominant Environmental Force Affect Your Objective(s)? (YES OR NO) **YES**

Probability [HIGH/LOW] competitor will notice your moves: **HIGH**

COMMENTS: Assume that Mythical Air Bag Materials has a strategic capability rating of "5." The only question on the Strategic Capability form that Mythical Air Bag Materials received a "0" on was the following: "Is the organization making, or does it have the resources to make organization acquisitions?" And we will assume that Mythical Air Bag Materials can effectively respond to Competitor16's actions.

Fig. 6.48

Scenario and Simulation Analysis

SCENARIO 16 (continued)   **[SIMULATION FORM]**

(Take into account the environmental forces)

A. Competitor's Move(s):

   Check each of the following that apply to indicate what the competitor is doing or will likely do:

     lower/raise price ☒ specialize in a market ☐ be quality leader ☐ increase vertical integration ☐

     increase investment in technology ☒ achieve brand name ☐ add services ☐ collaborate ☐

     increase investment in marketing ☐

   Comments: **This competitor wants to be a low-price provider.**

B. Your Response:

   Check each of the following that apply to indicate what your response is:

     ignore ☐ accommodate ☐ exit the market ☐ lower/raise price ☐ specialize in a market ☐

     be quality leader ☐ increase vertical integration ☐ increase investment in technology ☒

     achieve brand name ☐ add services ☐ collaborate ☐ increase investment in marketing ☐

   Comments:

C. Competitor's Response:

   Check each of the following that apply to indicate what your competitor's response is:

     ignore ☐ accommodate ☐ exit the market ☐ lower/raise price ☐ specialize in a market ☐

     be quality leader ☐ increase vertical integration ☐ increase investment in technology ☒

     achieve brand name ☐ add services ☐ collaborate ☐ increase investment in marketing ☐

   Comments:

D. Your Response:

   Check each of the following that apply to indicate what your response is:

     ignore ☐ accommodate ☐ exit the market ☐ lower/raise price ☐ specialize in a market ☐

     be quality leader ☐ increase vertical integration ☐ increase investment in technology ☒

     achieve brand name ☐ add services ☐ collaborate ☒ increase investment in marketing ☐

E. Your strategy to address scenario: **Invest in technology; monitor the inventor look for collaborative opportunities.**

Fig. 6.49

193

Chapter 6

SCENARIO 17: Suing Another Competitor

Introduction: From Concept 17 above, we see that Competitor17 is suing another competitor for royalties. Assumptions and knowledge for this competitor are as follows:

- Competitor17 is suing another air bag systems organization for money owed for using one of Competitor17's patented products.

- The patented product is not air bag fabric.

- This organization wants to protect its current brand name I.D.

- This organization has a relatively high strategic capability.

- This organization will notice our moves.

We need to monitor this entire process because legal action can change the dynamics of an industry. Using the results of our environmental forces analysis, our analysis of **Mythical Air Bag Materials'** business objectives in chapter 5, and the comments above, we now complete our scenario and simulation analysis for Competitor17.

Based on the above assumptions, we concluded that Competitor17 is trying to maintain, and possibly improve, its brand name identification. The appropriate items supporting this objective are checked on the following three scenario-simulation pages. We also believe that this competitor will increase its investment in technology. So this item is checked on the simulation form (figure 6.52).

194

SCENARIO 17

COMPETITOR ACTIVITIES FORM

What is the competitor doing? Competitor17 is suing another competitor for royalties

COMPETITOR BUSINESS OBJECTIVES FORM

"COMPETITOR'S" BUSINESS OBJECTIVES **INDUSTRY:** AIR BAG SYSTEMS **COMPETITOR:** Competitor17 (supplier)	INDICATE COMPETITOR'S BUSINESS OBJECTIVE(S) WITH A CHECK MARK.
To achieve low-price position	☐
To specialize in a market or market segment	☐
To sell the Top Quality Product/Service (Low product defect or low service error rate)	☐
To achieve vertical integration	☐
To be the technological leader	☐
To obtain brand identification	☒
To add service to product line	☐

STRATEGIC CAPABILITY FORM

COMPETITOR STRATEGIC CAPABILITY PARAMETER ESTIMATION **INDUSTRY:** AIR BAG SYSTEMS **COMPETITOR:** Competitor17	INDICATE "1" FOR YES, OR "0" FOR NO.
Is there enough demand for the product or service to support the existing competitors?	1
Is the organization making, or can it make an investment in technology?	1
Is the organization making, or does it have the resources to make organization acquisitions?	
Is the organization forming, or does it have the potential to form alliances or engage in some type of collaboration?	
Is the organization bringing in, or can the organization bring in high-powered personnel or management talent?	1
Is the organization influencing, or can the organization influence market demand using its marketing strength or technology strength?	
TOTAL (STRATEGIC CAPABILITY):	3

Fig. 6.50

Chapter 6

SIMULATION INITIALIZATION FORM

COMPETITOR: Competitor17
    INDUSTRY: AIR BAG SYSTEMS

ASSUMPTIONS/KNOWLEDGE

Dominant Environmental Force(s) [Critical Success Factor(s)]: **Government**

Competitor's Move(s): **Competitor17 Is Suing a Competitor for Royalties**

Precise Competitor's Business Objective(s): **To Achieve Brand Identification and Protect Brand Name**

Competitor's Strategic Capability (1-6, 6 being highest. Do scenario, if sc >= 3): **3**
[Build scenarios for organizations with sc >=3]

Your Organization's Business Objective(s): **To Be Technological Leader in Air Bag Fabrics**

Does Dominant Environmental Force Affect Your Competitor's Objective(s)? (YES OR NO) **Yes**

Does Dominant Environmental Force Affect Your Objective(s)? (YES OR NO) **Yes**

Probability [HIGH/LOW] competitor will notice your moves: **HIGH**

COMMENTS: Assume that Mythical Air Bag Materials has a strategic capability rating of "5." The only question on the Strategic Capability form that Mythical Air Bag Materials received a "0" on was the following: "Is the organization making, or does it have the resources to make organization acquisitions?" And we will assume that Mythical Air Bag Materials can effectively respond to Competitor17's actions.

Fig. 6.51

Scenario and Simulation Analysis

SCENARIO 17 (continued)   **[SIMULATION FORM]**

(Take into account the environmental forces)

A. Competitor's Move(s):

Check each of the following that apply to indicate what the competitor is doing or will likely do:

lower/raise price ☐ specialize in a market ☐ be quality leader ☐ increase vertical integration ☐

increase investment in technology ☒ achieve brand name ☒ add services ☐ collaborate ☐

increase investment in marketing ☐

Comments: **Competitor17 will use money to invest in technology; protect intellectual property.**

B. Your Response:

Check each of the following that apply to indicate what your response is:

ignore ☐ accommodate ☐ exit the market ☐ lower/raise price ☐ specialize in a market ☐

be quality leader ☐ increase vertical integration ☐ increase investment in technology ☒

achieve brand name ☐ add services ☐ collaborate ☐ increase investment in marketing ☐

Comments:

C. Competitor's Response:

Check each of the following that apply to indicate what your competitor's response is:

ignore ☒ accommodate ☐ exit the market ☐ lower/raise price ☐ specialize in a market ☐

be quality leader ☐ increase vertical integration ☐ increase investment in technology ☐

achieve brand name ☐ add services ☐ collaborate ☐ increase investment in marketing ☐

Comments:

D. Your Response:

Check each of the following that apply to indicate what your response is:

ignore ☐ accommodate ☐ exit the market ☐ lower/raise price ☐ specialize in a market ☐

be quality leader ☐ increase vertical integration ☐ increase investment in technology ☒

achieve brand name ☐ add services ☐ collaborate ☐ increase investment in marketing ☐

E. Your strategy to address scenario: **Invest in technology; monitor competitor.**

Fig. 6.52

197

Chapter 6

SCENARIO 18: A New Factory

Introduction: From Concept 18 above, we see that Competitor18 is constructing a new factory to build air bag systems components. Assumptions and knowledge for this competitor are as follows:

- This organization will not produce air bag fabric.

- This organization wants to bring more of its operations in-house.

- This organization has a relatively high strategic capability.

- This organization will notice our moves.

We need to see how the components they build will work with our fabric. Using the results of our environmental forces analysis, our analysis of **Mythical Air Bag Materials'** business objectives in chapter 5, and the comments above, we now complete our scenario and simulation analysis for Competitor18.

Based on the above assumptions, we decided that Competitor18 is bringing more of its air bag systems components production in-house. It is thus assumed that vertical integration is the competitor's main objective. Therefore, items on the following scenario-simulation pages that support this objective are checked.

SCENARIO 18

COMPETITOR ACTIVITIES FORM

What is the competitor doing? Building new factory to produce air bag system components

COMPETITOR BUSINESS OBJECTIVES FORM

"COMPETITOR'S" BUSINESS OBJECTIVES **INDUSTRY:** AIR BAG SYSTEMS **COMPETITOR:** Competitor18 (supplier)	INDICATE COMPETITOR'S BUSINESS OBJECTIVE(S) WITH A CHECK MARK.
To achieve low-price position	☐
To specialize in a market or market segment	☐
To sell the Top Quality Product/Service (Low product defect or low service error rate)	☐
To achieve vertical integration	☒
To be the technological leader	☐
To obtain brand identification	☐
To add service to product line	☐

STRATEGIC CAPABILITY FORM

COMPETITOR STRATEGIC CAPABILITY PARAMETER ESTIMATION **INDUSTRY:** AIR BAG SYSTEMS **COMPETITOR:** Competitor18	INDICATE "1" FOR YES, OR "0" FOR NO.
Is there enough demand for the product or service to support the existing competitors?	1
Is the organization making, or can it make an investment in technology?	1
Is the organization making, or does it have the resources to make organization acquisitions?	
Is the organization forming, or does it have the potential to form alliances or engage in some type of collaboration?	
Is the organization bringing in, or can the organization bring in high-powered personnel or management talent?	1
Is the organization influencing, or can the organization influence market demand using its marketing strength or technology strength?	
TOTAL (STRATEGIC CAPABILITY):	3

Fig. 6.53

Chapter 6

SIMULATION INITIALIZATION FORM

COMPETITOR: Competitor18
   INDUSTRY: AIR BAG SYSTEMS

ASSUMPTIONS/KNOWLEDGE

Dominant Environmental Force(s) [Critical Success Factor(s)]: **Government**

Competitor's Move(s): **Competitor18 is Building a New Factory**

Precise Competitor's Business Objective(s): **To Achieve Vertical Integration in Air Bag Systems**

Competitor's Strategic Capability (1-6, 6 being highest. Do scenario, if sc >= 3): **3**
[Build scenarios for organizations with sc >=3]

Your Organization's Business Objective(s): **To Be Technological Leader in Air Bag Fabrics**

Does Dominant Environmental Force Affect Your Competitor's Objective(s)? (YES OR NO) **YES**

Does Dominant Environmental Force Affect Your Objective(s)? (YES OR NO) **YES**

Probability [HIGH/LOW] competitor will notice your moves: **HIGH**

COMMENTS: Assume that Mythical Air Bag Materials has a strategic capability rating of "5." The only question on the Strategic Capability form that Mythical Air Bag Materials received a "0" on was the following: "Is the organization making, or does it have the resources to make organization acquisitions?" And we will assume that Mythical Air Bag Materials can effectively respond to Competitor18's actions.

Fig. 6.54

Scenario and Simulation Analysis

SCENARIO 18 (continued)   **[SIMULATION FORM]**

(Take into account the environmental forces)

A. Competitor's Move(s):

Check each of the following that apply to indicate what the competitor is doing or will likely do:

lower/raise price ☐ specialize in a market ☐ be quality leader ☐ increase vertical integration ☒

increase investment in technology ☐ achieve brand name ☐ add services ☐ collaborate ☐

increase investment in marketing ☐

Comments:

B. Your Response:

Check each of the following that apply to indicate what your response is:

ignore ☐ accommodate ☐ exit the market ☐ lower/raise price ☐ specialize in a market ☐

be quality leader ☐ increase vertical integration ☐ increase investment in technology ☒

achieve brand name ☐ add services ☐ collaborate ☐ increase investment in marketing ☐

Comments:

C. Competitor's Response:

Check each of the following that apply to indicate what your competitor's response is:

ignore ☐ accommodate ☐ exit the market ☐ lower/raise price ☐ specialize in a market ☐

be quality leader ☐ increase vertical integration ☒ increase investment in technology ☐

achieve brand name ☐ add services ☐ collaborate ☐ increase investment in marketing ☐

Comments:

D. Your Response:

Check each of the following that apply to indicate what your response is:

ignore ☐ accommodate ☐ exit the market ☐ lower/raise price ☐ specialize in a market ☐

be quality leader ☐ increase vertical integration ☐ increase investment in technology ☐

achieve brand name ☐ add services ☐ collaborate ☒ increase investment in marketing ☒

E. Your strategy to address scenario: **Invest in technology; monitor competitor; try to collaborate, if possible and appropriate.**

Fig. 6.55

Chapter 6

SCENARIO 19: Air Bag Fabric Maker

Introduction: From Concept 19 above, we see that Competitor19, a direct rival, has an agreement with a competitor (supplier) to make advanced air bags. Assumptions and knowledge for this competitor are as follows:

- This organization provides air bag fabric to organizations that make smaller air bags.

- This organization's fabric is used on air bags that use smart technology.

- This organization wants to be a leader in technology.

- This organization has a relatively high strategic capability.

- This organization will notice our moves.

We need to determine if there is some new fabric technology we do not know about. We need to see if we can differentiate our fabric. Using the results of our environmental forces analysis, our analysis of **Mythical Air Bag Materials'** business objectives in chapter 5, and the comments above, we now complete our scenario and simulation analysis for Competitor19.

Based on the above assumptions, we concluded that Competitor19 desires to be a leader in technology. We also feel that the organization will collaborate with certain organizations. Items which support this belief are checked on the simulation form (figure 6.58).

SCENARIO 19

COMPETITOR ACTIVITIES FORM

What is the competitor doing? Competitor makes air bag fabrics and is in agreement with air bag system supplier to develop advanced air bags

COMPETITOR BUSINESS OBJECTIVES FORM

"COMPETITOR'S" BUSINESS OBJECTIVES INDUSTRY: AIR BAG SYSTEMS COMPETITOR: Competitor19 (rival)	INDICATE COMPETITOR'S BUSINESS OBJECTIVE(S) WITH A CHECK MARK.
To achieve low-price position	☐
To specialize in a market or market segment	☐
To sell the Top Quality Product/Service (Low product defect or low service error rate)	☐
To achieve vertical integration	☐
To be the technological leader	☒
To obtain brand identification	☐
To add service to product line	☐

STRATEGIC CAPABILITY FORM

COMPETITOR STRATEGIC CAPABILITY PARAMETER ESTIMATION INDUSTRY: AIR BAG SYSTEMS COMPETITOR: Competitor19	INDICATE "1" FOR YES, OR "0" FOR NO.
Is there enough demand for the product or service to support the existing competitors?	1
Is the organization making, or can it make an investment in technology?	1
Is the organization making, or does it have the resources to make organization acquisitions?	
Is the organization forming, or does it have the potential to form alliances or engage in some type of collaboration?	1
Is the organization bringing in, or can the organization bring in high-powered personnel or management talent?	
Is the organization influencing, or can the organization influence market demand using its marketing strength or technology strength?	
TOTAL (STRATEGIC CAPABILITY):	3

Fig. 6.56

Chapter 6

SIMULATION INITIALIZATION FORM

COMPETITOR: Competitor19
    INDUSTRY: AIR BAG SYSTEMS

ASSUMPTIONS/KNOWLEDGE

Dominant Environmental Force(s) [Critical Success Factor(s)]: **Government**

Competitor's Move(s): **Competitor19 (rival) in Agreement with Competitor to Develop Advanced Air Bags**

Precise Competitor's Business Objective(s): **Technological Leader in Air Bag Fabric**

Competitor's Strategic Capability (1-6, 6 being highest. Do scenario, if sc >= 3): **3**
[Build scenarios for organizations with sc >=3]

Your Organization's Business Objective(s):   **To Be Technological Leader in Air Bag Fabrics**

Does Dominant Environmental Force Affect Your Competitor's Objective(s)? (YES OR NO) **YES**

Does Dominant Environmental Force Affect Your Objective(s)? (YES OR NO) **YES**

Probability [HIGH/LOW] competitor will notice your moves: **HIGH**

COMMENTS: Assume that Mythical Air Bag Materials has a strategic capability rating of "5." The only question on the Strategic Capability form that Mythical Air Bag Materials received a "0" on was the following: "Is the organization making, or does it have the resources to make organization acquisitions?" And we will assume that Mythical Air Bag Materials can effectively respond to Competitor19's actions.

Fig. 6.57

SCENARIO 19 (continued)　　　　　**[SIMULATION FORM]**

(Take into account the environmental forces)

A. Competitor's Move(s):

　Check each of the following that apply to indicate what the competitor is doing or will likely do:

　　lower/raise price ☐　specialize in a market ☐　be quality leader ☐　increase vertical integration ☐

　　increase investment in technology ☒　achieve brand name ☐　add services ☐　collaborate ☒

　　increase investment in marketing ☐

　Comments:　**Try to get a sample of the competitor's fabric.**

B. Your Response:

　Check each of the following that apply to indicate what your response is:

　　ignore ☐　accommodate ☐　exit the market ☐　lower/raise price ☐　specialize in a market ☒

　　be quality leader ☐　increase vertical integration ☐　increase investment in technology ☐

　　achieve brand name ☐　add services ☐　collaborate ☐　increase investment in marketing ☐

　Comments:　**Determine if our fabric is superior to the competitor's.**

C. Competitor's Response:

　Check each of the following that apply to indicate what your competitor's response is:

　　ignore ☐　accommodate ☐　exit the market ☐　lower/raise price ☐　specialize in a market ☐

　　be quality leader ☐　increase vertical integration ☐　increase investment in technology ☐

　　achieve brand name ☐　add services ☐　collaborate ☒　increase investment in marketing ☐

　Comments:　**Learn more about the agreement.**

D. Your Response:

　Check each of the following that apply to indicate what your response is:

　　ignore ☐　accommodate ☐　exit the market ☐　lower/raise price ☐　specialize in a market ☒

　　be quality leader ☐　increase vertical integration ☐　increase investment in technology ☒

　　achieve brand name ☐　add services ☐　collaborate ☐　increase investment in marketing ☐

E. Your strategy to address scenario: **Continue to invest in technology; differentiate our product; find out more about the fabric used by our competitor.**

Fig. 6.58

Chapter 6

SCENARIO 20: Child Seat Protection

Introduction: From Concept 20 above, we see that Competitor20 has developed a child seat to protect kids from inflating air bags. Assumptions and knowledge for this competitor are as follows:

- This organization has invested heavily in research and development.

- This child seat technology might work better with some air bag fabrics than with others.

- Some types of air bags appear to cause more injuries to children than other types.

- This organization has a relatively high strategic capability.

- This organization will notice our moves.

Some air bags appear to cause injuries, whereas other air bags appear not to cause injuries. We want to monitor the investigations of these injuries. If it turns out that some air bags work better with this child seat, we want to make sure we are associated with that air bag supplier.

Using the results of our environmental forces analysis, our analysis of **Mythical Air Bag Materials'** business objectives in chapter 5, and the comments above, we now complete our scenario and simulation analysis for Competitor20.

Based on the above assumptions, and the fact that Competitor20 is specializing in the child seat protection area, we concluded that this competitor's main objective is to specialize in the child seat market. Items supporting this objective are checked on the following three scenario-simulation pages. Since we believe that the competitor will increase its investment in technology, we indicate this on the simulation form (figure 6.61).

SCENARIO 20

COMPETITOR ACTIVITIES FORM

What is the competitor doing? Developing child seat designed to deflect force of inflating air bag away from child

COMPETITOR BUSINESS OBJECTIVES FORM

"COMPETITOR'S" BUSINESS OBJECTIVES INDUSTRY: AIR BAG SYSTEMS COMPETITOR: Competitor20 (supplier)	INDICATE COMPETITOR'S BUSINESS OBJECTIVE(S) WITH A CHECK MARK.
To achieve low-price position	☐
To specialize in a market or market segment	☒
To sell the Top Quality Product/Service (Low product defect or low service error rate)	☐
To achieve vertical integration	☐
To be the technological leader	☐
To obtain brand identification	☐
To add service to product line	☐

STRATEGIC CAPABILITY FORM

COMPETITOR STRATEGIC CAPABILITY PARAMETER ESTIMATION INDUSTRY: AIR BAG SYSTEMS COMPETITOR: Competitor20	INDICATE "1" FOR YES, OR "0" FOR NO.
Is there enough demand for the product or service to support the existing competitors?	1
Is the organization making, or can it make an investment in technology?	1
Is the organization making, or does it have the resources to make organization acquisitions?	
Is the organization forming, or does it have the potential to form alliances or engage in some type of collaboration?	1
Is the organization bringing in, or can the organization bring in high-powered personnel or management talent?	
Is the organization influencing, or can the organization influence market demand using its marketing strength or technology strength?	
TOTAL (STRATEGIC CAPABILITY):	3

Fig. 6.59

SCENARIO 20 (continued)

SIMULATION INITIALIZATION FORM

COMPETITOR: Competitor20
    INDUSTRY: AIR BAG SYSTEMS

ASSUMPTIONS/KNOWLEDGE

Dominant Environmental Force(s) [Critical Success Factor(s)]: **Government**

Competitor's Move(s): **Developed Child Seat Designed to Deflect Force of Inflating Air Bag Away from Child**

Precise Competitor's Business Objective(s): **To Specialize in Child Seat Market**

Competitor's Strategic Capability (1-6, 6 being highest. Do scenario, if sc >= 3): **3**
[Build scenarios for organizations with sc >=3]

Your Organization's Business Objective(s): **To Be Technological Leader in Air Bag Fabrics**

Does Dominant Environmental Force Affect Your Competitor's Objective(s)? (YES OR NO) **YES**

Does Dominant Environmental Force Affect Your Objective(s)? **(YES OR NO) YES**

Probability [HIGH/LOW] competitor will notice your moves: **HIGH**

COMMENTS: Assume that Mythical Air Bag Materials has a strategic capability rating of "5." The only question on the Strategic Capability form that Mythical Air Bag Materials received a "0" on was the following: "Is the organization making, or does it have the resources to make organization acquisitions?" And we will assume that Mythical Air Bag Materials can effectively respond to Competitor20's actions.

Fig. 6.60

Scenario and Simulation Analysis

SCENARIO 20 (continued)   **[SIMULATION FORM]**

(Take into account the environmental forces)

A. Competitor's Move(s):

    Check each of the following that apply to indicate what the competitor is doing or will likely do:

      lower/raise price ☐   specialize in a market ☒   be quality leader ☐   increase vertical integration ☐

      increase investment in technology ☒   achieve brand name ☐   add services ☐   collaborate ☐

      increase investment in marketing ☐

    Comments: **Make sure we supply fabric to suppliers that make safe air bags.**

B. Your Response:

    Check each of the following that apply to indicate what your response is:

      ignore ☐   accommodate ☐   exit the market ☐   lower/raise price ☐   specialize in a market ☐

      be quality leader ☐   increase vertical integration ☐   increase investment in technology ☒

      achieve brand name ☐   add services ☐   collaborate ☐   increase investment in marketing ☒

    Comments: **We can approach this competitor with a collaboration offer.**

C. Competitor's Response:

    Check each of the following that apply to indicate what your competitor's response is:

      ignore ☐   accommodate ☐   exit the market ☐   lower/raise price ☐   specialize in a market ☐

      be quality leader ☐   increase vertical integration ☐   increase investment in technology ☐

      achieve brand name ☐   add services ☐   collaborate ☒   increase investment in marketing ☐

    Comments:

D. Your Response:

    Check each of the following that apply to indicate what your response is:

      ignore ☐   accommodate ☐   exit the market ☐   lower/raise price ☐   specialize in a market ☐

      be quality leader ☐   increase vertical integration ☐   increase investment in technology ☒

      achieve brand name ☐   add services ☐   collaborate ☒ increase investment in marketing ☐

E. Your strategy to address scenario: **Invest in technology; determine if our organization can supply fabric to the child seat manufacturers.**

Fig. 6.61

Chapter 6

Business Strategy Considerations

Below is the **FINAL STRATEGY FORM**. As you can see, on this form we indicate our beliefs about the environmental forces, and we show what our business strategy should be for a planning period. It should be noted that this type of scenario-simulation exercise should be carried out periodically. Engaging in this type of exercise will enable an organization to better anticipate, detect and respond to changes in the business environment. Thus, engaging in this type of exercise will enable an organization to enhance its strategic management.

FINAL STRATEGY FORM

DATE: 07 /01 /98

YOUR ORGANIZATION NAME: **MYTHICAL AIR BAG MATERIALS**

DOMINANT FORCE (S): **GOVERNMENT (TECHNOLOGY TO LESSER DEGREE)**

COMPETITOR (S): **AIR BAG SYSTEMS ORGANIZATIONS**

CHOSEN STRATEGY: **CONTINUE WITH INVESTMENT IN TECHNOLOGY; MONITOR COMPETITORS AND THE GOVERNMENT; COLLABORATE**

DOES THIS STRATEGY TAKE ADVANTAGE OF THE DOMINANT FORCE?   YES ☒ NO ☐

DOES THE DOMINANT FORCE THREATEN YOUR CHOSEN STRATEGY?   YES ☐ NO ☒

COMMENTS:

Fig. 6.62

SUMMARY

Scenario and simulation methods can be used to analyze competitors' current and possible future activities within an assumed current and future business environment. Competitor-related concepts describing a competitor's activities should first be determined. Once the competitor's activities are appropriately identified, and intelligence associated with the competitor's objectives and strategic capability has been obtained, scenarios can be established.

A scenario-simulation exercise can be completed using this information as input to a set of forms. These forms allow manual simulation of competitive situations. The forms are as follows: the COMPETITOR ACTIVITIES FORM, the COMPETITOR BUSINESS OBJECTIVE FORM, the STRATEGIC CAPABILITY FORM, the SIMULATION INITIALIZATION FORM, the SIMULATION FORM, and the FINAL STRATEGY FORM. After the simulation is completed, a business strategy that exploits business opportunities and avoids threats to an organization can be established. Reviewing and refining this business strategy should be an ongoing activity for effective strategic management.

Afterword

This book is about examining business environmental information to gain opportunity and threat insight. We view business intelligence as information that can help provide this insight. Furthermore, we view business intelligence as a key element in strategic management.

This book described text mining as a way to perform environmental scanning, and scenario and simulation analysis as a method to perform competitor analysis. We defined ten key environmental force types. We discussed information extraction as a special form of text mining. And we emphasized that information extraction is a way to identify and extract predetermined business concepts. Also, we used visualization methods to examine environmental forces for business intelligence. We analyzed business concepts and showed how these concepts can be converted into business intelligence.

We discussed online systems and online systems' content. We noted that some online systems provide access to text amenable to the application of text mining methods. Selected online systems contain large quantities of text that we can screen to identify that which conforms to domain requirements. We can "mine" and analyze this text for opportunities and threats.

We discussed dominant environmental forces associated with the air bag systems industry over a ten-year period. We created and analyzed environmental forces visualization charts and we analyzed associated concepts. We assumed a future environment based on the results of our analysis.

We introduced two methods for identifying concepts that contain strategically capable competitors. We also introduced a method for measuring an organization's strategic capability.

We introduced analysis methods, employing forms to facilitate the analysis. We used the forms to analyze the air bag systems industry, examine the business environment, and identify organization objectives and competitor actions. We performed these analyses from the perspective of a fictional organization called **Mythical Air Bag Materials**. We used scenario and simulation analysis methods to examine the fictional organization's responses to competitor activities. And finally, we chose business strategies for the fictional organization, based on the scenario-simulation analyses.

The author sincerely hopes that this book has helped the reader better understand text mining and business information analysis. The author hopes that the reader understands how text mining and scenario and simulation analysis can help an organization examine the environment and competitor activities. And the author hopes that the reader has gained some insight into how business information can be converted into business intelligence that can help an organization improve its strategic management.

Bibliography

Adriaans, Pieter and Dolf Zantinge. *Data Mining*. Reading, Massachusetts: Addison-Wesley, 1996.

Aguilar, Francis J. *Scanning the Business Environment*. New York: The Macmillan Company, 1967.

Beckwith, Harry. *Selling the Invisible: A Field Guide to Modern Marketing*. New York: Warner Books, 1997.

Cabena, Peter, Pablo Hadjinian, Rolf Stadler, Jaap Verhees, and Alessandro Zanasi. *Discovering Data Mining: From Concepts to Implementation*. Upper Saddler River, New Jersey: Prentice Hall PTR, 1997.

Choo, Chun Wei. *Information Management for the Intelligent Organization: The Art of Scanning the Environment*. Medford, New Jersey: Information Today, Inc., 2002

Day, George S., David J. Reibstein and Robert E. Gunther. *Wharton on Dynamic Competitive Strategy*. New York: John Wiley & Sons, 1997.

Fahey, Liam and Robert M. Randall. *Learning from the Future: Competitive Foresight Scenarios*. New York: John Wiley & Sons, 1997.

Fahy, Martin. *Strategic Enterprise Management: Tools for the 21ˢᵗ Century*. London: CIMA Publishing, 2002.

Fuld, Leonard M. *The New Competitor Intelligence: The Complete Resource for Finding, Analyzing, and Using Information about Your Competitors*. New York: John Wiley & Sons, 1994.

Georgantzas, Nicholas C., and William Acar. *Scenario-Driven Planning: Learning to Manage Strategic Uncertainty*. Westport, Connecticut: Greenwood Publishing Group, 1995.

Gilad, Ben and Jan P. Herring. *The Art and Science of Business Intelligence Analysis: Business Intelligence Theory, Principles, Practices, and Uses*. Greenwich, Connecticut: JAI Press, 1996.

Gilad, Ben and Jan P. Herring. *The Art and Science of Business Intelligence Analysis: Intelligence Analysis and Its Applications*. Greenwich, Connecticut: JAI Press, 1996.

Bibliography

Howson, Cindi. *Successful Business Intelligence: Secrets to Making BI a Killer App.* New York: McGraw-Hill Osborne Media, 2007.

Kleiner, Art. "Database." 1999 Grolier Multimedia Encyclopedia. Deluxe ed. Danbury, Connecticut: Grolier Interactive, 1998.

Kotler, Philip. *Kotler On Marketing: How to Create, Win and Dominate Markets.* New York: The Free Press, 1999.

Lavin, Michael R. *Business Information: How to Find It, How to Use It.* 2d ed. Phoenix, Arizona: The Oryx Press, 1992.

Luhn, H. P. "A Business Intelligence System." IBM Journal, 1958.

Maddux, David. *1999 Editor & Publisher International Year Book.* 79th ed. New York: Editor & Publisher Company, 1999.

McCarthy, Joseph F. "A Trainable Approach to Coreference Resolution for Information Extraction." Ph.D. diss., University of Massachusetts Amherst, 1996.

Merrill, John C. "Newspaper." 1999 Grolier Multimedia Encyclopedia. Deluxe ed. Danbury, Connecticut: Grolier Interactive, 1998.

Oskamp, Stuart. "Opinion Polls." 1999 Grolier Multimedia Encyclopedia. Deluxe ed. Danbury, Connecticut: Grolier Interactive, 1998.

Popovich, Charles J. *Business and Economics Databases Online: Environmental Scanning With a Personal Computer (Advanced Online Searching Series).* Littleton, Colorado: Libraries Unlimited, 1987.

Porter, Michael E. *Competitive Strategy: Techniques for Analyzing Industries and Competitors.* New York: The Free Press, 1980.

Renfro, William L. *Issues Management in Strategic Planning.* Westport, Connecticut: Quorum Books, 1993.

Riloff, Ellen M. "Information Extraction as a Basis for Portable Text Classification Systems." Ph.D. diss., University of Massachusetts Amherst, 1994.

Robert, Michael. *Strategy Pure & Simple: How Winning CEOs Outthink Their Competition.* McGraw-Hill, Inc., 1993.

Bibliography

Schwartz, Peter. *The Art of the Long View: Planning for the Future in an Uncertain World.* New York: Doubleday, 1991.

Scrage, Michael. *Serious Play: How the World's Best Companies Simulate to Innovate.* Boston, Massachusetts: Harvard Business School Press, 1999.

Stoffels, John D. *Strategic Issues Management: A Comprehensive Guide to Environmental Scanning.* Oxford, Ohio: The Planning Forum, 1994.

Subramanian, R., K. Kumar, and C. Yauger. "The Scanning of Task Environments in Hospitals: An Empirical Study." Journal of Applied Business Research, Vol 10, Issue 4: p104, 1994.

Swayne, Linda E., Jack Duncan, and Peter M. Ginter. *Strategic Management of Health Care Organizations.* Wiley-Blackwell, 2007.

Tang, Victor and Roy Bauer. *Competitive Dominance: Beyond Strategic Advantage and Total Quality Management.* New York: Van Nostrand Reinhold, 1995.

Treacy, Michael and Fred Wiersema. *The Discipline of Market Leaders: Choose Your Customers, Narrow Your Focus, Dominate Your Market.* Cambridge, Massachusetts: Perseus Books, 1995.

Usama, Fayyad M., Gregory Piatetsky-Shapiro, Padhraic Smyth and Ramasamy Uthurusamy. *Advances in Knowledge Discovery and Data Mining.* Menlo Park, California: AAAI Press / The MIT Press, 1996.

Weiss, Sholom M. and Nitin Indurkhya. *Predictive Data Mining: A Practical Guide.* San Francisco, California: Morgan Kaufmann Publishers, 1997.

Index

Index

Index

Printed in the United States
211678BV00001B/1/P

9 780967 490663